The great metropolis of Los Angeles proves vastly more complex and sophisticated than its Hollywood image. Layered and diverse, the city of palm trees and sunshine enjoys its coastal location while remaining just an hour's drive from snow capped mountains and expansive deserts. Cheaper than New York and with better weather, Los Angeles acts as a hub for thriving international art, architecture, nightlight, and culinary scenes. The infectious optimism found in this unique and surprisingly unpretentious city will make you wonder why you live anywhere else.

CITIx60: Los Angeles explores the world's film capital and the largest city in the state of California in five aspects, covering architecture, art spaces, shops and markets, eating and entertainment. With expert advice from 60 stars of the city's creative scene, this book guides you to the real attractions of the city for an authentic taste of Los Angeles life.

Contents

W9-CFI-974

Before You Go

BASIC INFO

Currency
U.S. Dollar (USD/$)
Exchange rate: $1 : €0.7

Time zone
GMT −8
DST −7

DST begins at 0200 (local time) on the second Sunday of March and ends at 0300 (local time) on the first Sunday of November.

Dialling
International calling: +1
Citywide: 213, 310, 323, 424, 626, 818, 661, 747

*Always include area code for calls. Dial 1 for domestic calls, or 001 for calls made outside the US.

Weather (avg. temperature range)
Spring (Mar–May): 9–20°C / 48–68°F
Summer (Jun–Sep): 15–25°C / 59–77°F
Autumn (Oct–Nov): 11–23°C / 52–73°F
Winter (Dec–Feb): 7–17°C / 45–63°F

USEFUL WEBSITES

LA Bike Paths
www.labikepaths.com

Visa application
travel.state.gov/content/visas/english.html

EMERGENCY CALLS

Ambulance, fire or police
911

Non-emergency police
+1 (877) 275 5273

Consulates
China   +1 (213) 807 8088
Japan   +1 (213) 617 6700
France   +1 (310) 235 3200
Germany   +1 (323) 930 2703
UK   +1 (310) 481 0031

AIRPORT EXPRESS TRANSFER

LAX Airport <-> Union Station (LAX FlyAway)
Bus / Journey: every 20–60 mins / 35 mins
From LAX T1 – 1200–2330
(allow extra time for T2-7 pick-up)
From Union Station – 1200–2330
One-way: $8
www.lawa.org/FlyAway

PUBLIC TRANSPORT IN LOS ANGELES

Metro Rail
Metro Bus
DASH
Taxi

Means of payment
TAP card
Cash
Credit cards

PUBLIC HOLIDAYS

January	1 New Year's Day, Martin Luther King Jr. Day (3rd Mon)
February	Presidents' Day (3rd Mon)
March	30 César Chávez Day
May	Memorial Day (Last Mon)
July	4 Independence Day
September	Labour Day (1st Mon)
October	Columbus Day (2nd Mon)
November	General Election Day (Tue after 1st Mon)**, 11 Veterans Day, Thanksgiving Day & the following day (4th Thu & Fri)
December	25 Christmas Day

* If a holiday falls on a weekend, the closest weekday becomes a 'substitute' day. ** Date of holiday is observed only in election years. Museums, galleries and shops are likely to be closed or operate on special hours on Thanksgiving, Christmas Eve, Christmas Day, New Year's Day, and Independence Day.

FESTIVALS / EVENTS

January
LA Art Show
www.laartshow.com
LA Art Book Fair
www.laartbookfair.net

February
The Academy Awards (or March)
oscar.go.com

March
Burgerama
burgerrecords.tumblr.com
Los Angeles Marathon
www.lamarathon.com

April
Coachella
www.coachella.com
UCLA Jazz Reggae Festival
www.jazzreggaefest.com

June
LA Pride
lapride.org
Los Angeles Film Festival
www.lafilmfest.com

July
Outfest
www.outfest.org

August
The Great Gatsby Party
www.drinkeatplay.com/gatsby

September
Abbot Kinney Festival (or October)
www.abbotkinney.org
SCI-Arc Graduate Thesis Reviews
www.sciarc.edu

October
Screamfest Horror Film Festival
screamfestla.com

Event days vary by year. Please check for
updates online.

UNUSUAL OUTINGS

LA River Bird Walk & Night Runs
playthelariver.com

Fantastic Race
www.amazinglarace.com

Dearly Departed Tours
dearlydepartedtours.com

Downtown Artwalk
www.downtownartwalk.org

Conservancy's Walking Tour
www.laconservancy.org

SMARTPHONE APP

Reserve / request a ride in no time
Curb

Request a for-hire driver & pay through app
Uber
Lyft

Daily cue for urban exploration
5 Every Day

REGULAR EXPENSES

Newspaper
$2–5

Domestic / International mail (postcards)
$0.49/$1.15

Gratuities
Diners: 15–20% for waitstaff & bartenders
Hotels: $1–2@bag for porter, $1–5 daily for
cleaners
Licensed taxis: 15–20%

Count to 10

What makes Los Angeles so special?
Illustrations by Guillaume Kashima aka Funny Fun

People flock to Los Angeles for the unbeatable weather but stay for its rich cultural value. From avant-garde and modern architectural gems to a thriving culinary scene and invigorating outdoor activities, the city maintains a diverse and lasting appeal. Whether you are on a one-day stopover or a week-long stay, see what Los Angeles creatives consider essential to see, taste, read and take home from your trip.

1

Architecture

Emerson College Los Angeles
by Morphosis Architects

Ramon C. Cortines School of Visual and Performing Arts
by CoopHimmelb(l)au

Cathedral of Our Lady of the Angels
by Rafael Moneo

Coca-Cola Building
by Robert V. Derrah

The Bullocks Wilshire
by John & Donald Parkinson

The Millard House
by Frank Lloyd Wright

The Donut Hole
by John Tindall, Ed McCreany & Jesse Hood

Walt Disney Concert Hall
by Frank Gehry

2
Designer Houses

Lovell House
by Richard Neutra

Stahl House
by Pierre Koenig

Malin Residence (Chemosphere)
by John Lautner

Sheats Goldstein Residence
by John Lautner

Gamble House
by Greene and Greene

Schindler House (#4)
by Rudolph & Pauline Schindler

Eames House (#5)
*by Eero Saarinen,
Charles Eames*

Al Struckus House (#8)
by Bruce Goff

3
Select Shops & Shopping Districts

Hennessey + Ingalls
www.hennesseyingalls.com

Arcana Books on the Arts
www.arcanabooks.com

Poketo
www.poketo.com

Creatures of Comfort LA
www.creaturesofcomfort.us

Polkadots & Moonbeams
polkadotsandmoonbeams.com

Abbot Kinney Boulevard
abbotkinneyblvd.com

Main Street, Saint Monica
www.mainstreetsm.com

Sportie LA Sneakers
sportiela.com

4
Mexican Delight

Chorizo mulita
Taco Zone
*1342 N. Alvarado St. & Montana
St., CA 90027*

Blackjack quesadilla
Kogi
kogibbq.com

Aguacate frito
Cacao Mexicatessen
cacaodeli.com

**Homestyle braises on
handmade tortilla**
Guisados
www.guisados.co

Al pastor
La Reyna
7th St. & Mateo, CA 90021

Suadero taco
Bellevue Steakhouse
1415 Bellevue Ave., CA 90026

5

Burgers

Burger & apple pie
The Apple Pan
10801 W. Pico Blvd., CA 90064

Witte burger
Grill 'em All
grillemallburgs.com

Veggie burger
Café Gratitude LA
cafegratitude.com

Office burger
Father's Office
fathersoffice.com

Throwback burger
Umami Burger
www.umamiburger.com

5 oz. original burger
Mo Better Burgers
www.mobetterburgers.com

6

Staple Food

Godmother sandwich
Bay Cities Italian Deli & Bakery
www.baycitiesitaliandeli.com

**Hot Dog on a Stick
& Cherry Lemonade**
Hot Dog on a Stick
1633 Ocean Front Walk, CA 90401

Fleur de Sel Caramels
Valerie Confections
www.valerieconfections.com

"Salty Pimp" or "Bea Arthur"
Big Gay Ice Cream
biggayicecream.com

Coconut donut
Randy's Donuts
805 W. Manchester Ave., CA 90301

Michelada ice pop with beer
Diablo Taco
www.diablotaco.com

7

Hiking Spots

Visit the Hollywood Sign
Hollywood Hills

Wildflowers & waterfall
Eaton Canyon

Scenic view of Hollywood
Runyon Canyon Park

**Hiking, golf, pony rides
& more**
Griffith Park

Along ocean shoreline
Point Mugu State Park

Well-maintained city park
Elysian Park

Shaded canyon hike
Solstice Canyon Malibu

8

Hollywood Film Scene

Safari Inn
True Romance (1993)
by Tony Scott

Eastern Columbia Lofts
500 Days of Summer (2009)
by Marc Webb

Ennis House (#11)
Blade Runner (1982)
by Ridley Scott

Santa Monica Pier
Her (2013)
by Spike Jonze

Los Angeles River (#10)
Drive (2011)
by Nicolas Winding Refn

Sunset Boulevard
Sunset Boulevard (1950)
by Billy Wilder

9

Leisure

Go surfing
Malibu Lagoon State Beach

Street art hunting
Arts District by the likes of JR,
DabsMyla, How Nosm, Shepard
Fairey & Paige Smith

Watch The Room (2003)
Landmark Regent Theaters
monthly first Saturday

Music alfresco with picnic
Hollywood Bowl
www.hollywoodbowl.com

Visit Echo Park Lake
with a six-pack Tecate beer

**Behold massive lake with
post-apocalyptic scenery**
Bombay Beach

Have a Passion Fruit Mai Tai
Tonga Hut
www.tongahut.com

10

Day trip
*Recommended by
John Boiler, 72andSunny*

Start with a morning hike
Point Mugu State Park

Bike + fish sandwich
Neptune's Net (Pacific Coast Hwy)

**Check out Johnny Carson's &
celebrity houses**
Malibu Colony Rd., Malibu Creek

**Visit "Rome meets Hollywood"
sculpture gardens**
Getty Villa

A turn on the Ferris Wheel
Santa Monica Pier

Visit LA's first beach town
El Segundo

Have a schooner of beer
Richmond Bar & Grill, El Segundo

**Have burger @Simmzy's
or decent dinner @Fonz's**
Manhattan Beach

Icon Index

 Opening hours

 Admission

 Address

 Facebook

 Contact

URL Website

 Remarks

Scan QR codes to access Google Maps and discover the area around each destination. Internet connection required.

60x60

60 Local Creatives x 60 Hotspots

From vast cityscapes to the tiniest glimpses of everyday exchange, there is much to provoke one's imagination. 60x60 points you to 60 haunts where 60 arbiters of taste go for the good stuff.

Landmarks & Architecture
SPOTS · 01 – 12 📍

Hollywood stars aren't outshining any architectural legends. Rove the Case Study houses, landmark buildings and the hills to glimpse the city beyond the silver screen.

Cultural & Art Spaces
SPOTS · 13 – 24 📍

Soak up the creative energy from large scale installations to prints and art pieces as revered curators continually put up provocative shows and excellent archives.

Markets & Shops
SPOTS · 25 – 36 📍

Makers and shoppers find endless inspiration for wardrobe and lifestyle goods here. Abbot Kinney and Melrose are just some of the names to always keep in mind.

Restaurants & Cafés
SPOTS · 37 – 48 📍

From the curb to the coast, dawn to dusk, make the city's cultural diversity and home cooking one of your fond memories to take away.

Nightlife
SPOTS · 49 – 60 📍

Factor in the traffic before you go as punctuality saves you the best seats and ensures entry. Visitors of all ages will delight in the various activities that the city has to offer.

Landmarks & Architecture

Designer houses, cinematic locations, and the urban wilderness

The sky's the limit when it comes to Los Angeles' architectural legacy. For a city struggling to preserve its countless landmarks ahead of hungry developers, this town offers a wealth of architectural treasures encompassing the expansive, manmade Los Angeles River (#10), the more glamorous Hollywood Forever Cemetery and Chateau Marmont (#12), and a trove of residential projects both quirky and elegant. The Griffith Observatory (#1), an Art Deco masterpiece featured in countless films, can be glimpsed from far and wide thanks to its prominent location in the Hollywood Hills. With famed modernist architects from Frank Lloyd Wright to Rudolph Schindler and Richard Neutra fleeing harsh winters and spatial constraints from back east and Europe, the city hosts numerous seminal projects including Wright's Hollyhock (#6) and Ennis Houses (#11) as well as Schindler's personal home (#4). Exemplified by the Eames House (#5) designed by Ray and Charles Eames, The Case Study House Program during the 50's and 60's transformed LA into the mecca for the mid-century modernist movement.

Never get lost again in search of the Hollywood Sign by car, with Ben Mor's advice: put *Lake Hollywood Park, CA 90068* in your GPS, and start your trip at *Beachwood Canyon*. Go north all the way up hill till you get to *Ledgewood Drive* and make a *Left*. At the first fork in the road stay to the left. You're still on Ledgewood Drive, and as you cross *Mulholand Highway* stay to the right and now you will start driving downhill a bit. Continue till you see the dog park and the Hollywood sign nice and big on your right.

Lo-fang
Musician

I'm Matthew Hemerlein, a musician from Maryland, who moved to Los Angeles two years ago.

The Huntington Gardens P.016

CYRCLE.
Art collective

We are CYRCLE., an LA based art collective. We love to travel, but always enjoy coming home.

MI–ZO
Photographer & director unit

MI–ZO is composed of a photographer Zoren Gold and a graphic artist Minori Murakami. They've been based in New York, Tokyo and LA, working globally with advertising, art and film.

Griffith Observatory P.014

Neutra VDL Studio & Residences P.018

Thom Mayne
Founder, Morphsis Architect

After setting up Morphosis in 1972, Mayne co-founded SCI-Arc. He is also a professor at UCLA. His distinguished honors include the Pritzker Prize (2005) and the AIA Gold Medal (2013).

Eames House P.020

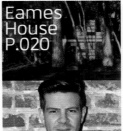

Patrick Hruby
Artist

Born in LA, but as a child I spent some time in a log cabin in Spirit Lake, Idaho. Obsessed with color and geometry. I teach at my alma mater, Art Center College of Design.

Shark Toof
Artist

I'm a native Angeleno raised on graffiti art. My work reflects the vibrancy of LA, encompassing nature, fashion, and Hollywood. All these aspects have shaped my career and my art.

Schindler House P.019

Hollyhock House P.021

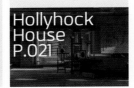

Neil Huxley
Director & creative director

An LA transplant but still a Londoner at heart, I am a commercial director at Mothership and creative director for Digital Domain. I also develop film projects with my writer brother Philip Huxley.

Al Struckus House
P.023

Ben Mor
Director

I am a Los Angeles based director. I make propaganda films for multinationals. I am also responsible for some of the top video clips/promos. Next stop – your local Multiplex.

Bobby Solomon
Founder, The Fox Is Black

Bobby Solomon is the founder and editor-in-chief of The Fox Is Black, a culture blog showcasing matters of design and design that matters.

Bradbury Building
P.022

Cinerama Dome
P.024

Gina Clyne
Photographer & designer

With a fine art photography background, I shoot events and collaborate with musicians on album art, posters and related ephemera. I'm also a book binder and avid plant collector.

Ennis House
P.026

Danny Boy O'Connor
Rapper & creative director

A founding member of hip hop groups House of Pain and La Coka Nostra. With Delta Bravo Urban Exploration Team, I am currently working from LA, New York, Boston, and Chicago.

Rich Sommer
Actor

I'm an actor, recently appeared on Mad Men. Like cocktails and board games. I'm from Minnesota, which explains my simple tastes.

Los Angeles River
P.025

Chateau Marmont
P.027

1 Griffith Observatory
Map D, P.100

Since 1935, this Art Deco complex has remained a captivating icon and learning facility for the city. The domed white structure, prominently placed in the hills above Los Feliz, stands as the visual counterpoint to the Hollywood sign and the backdrop to many classic films. A perfect destination for a hike, picnic, a day of science, or an evening under the stars, this elegant homage to the universe offers some of the best views of the metropolis free of charge.

🕐 1200–2200 (Tu–F), 1000– (Sa–Su)
🏠 2800 E. Observatory Rd., CA 90027
📞 +1 (213) 473 0800 URL www.griffithobs.org
📎 Check website for public holiday schedule

"I almost became an astronaut and this is the closest I've been able to get to feeling as though I'm in outer space as when I trained with NASA"
– Lo-fang

2 The Huntington Gardens
Map V, P.107

One of Southern California's most breathtaking gardens can be found just a 30-minute drive from Hollywood. Part of the sweeping grounds of the Huntington Library and Art Collections, the 12 botanical gardens meander over the 120-acre estate. The gardens feature over 15,000 plant varieties that showcase swatches of the world's ecosystems and a range of educational programs focused on sustainable urban agriculture. Highlights include the picturesque Rose Garden and the Garden of Flowering Fragrance.

🕐 1200-1630 (M, W-F), 1030- (Sa-Su), Summer hours (Memorial Day - Labour Day): 1030-1630 (W-M)
💲 $23/20/18/15/8
📍 1151 Oxford Rd., CA 91108
URL www.huntington.org

"From Japanese Gardens to desert landscapes, it's easy to spend an entire day there."
– CYRCLE.

3 Neutra VDL Studio & Residences

Map A1, P.109

Now one of the National Register of Historic Places, VDL studio was designed by Richard Neutra (1892–1970) with his son Dion (1926–) as an experiment of modern architecture and human psychology. The philosophy of this 2,100 square foot house focuses on precision. Playing with concepts of depth and social interaction, the modernist masterpiece gives the illusion of expansive space. Unusual for the time, raw materials from aluminum to mirror, steel, and glass work together to create the home's distinctive aesthetic.

🏠 *2300 Silver Lake Blvd., CA 90039*
URL *www.neutra-vdl.org*
🕒 *30-min guided tours: 1100–1500 (Sa). Last tour starts at 1430, $10*

"It's where Richard Neutra himself lived and worked. The house is kept amazingly well, it's a timeless beauty."

– MI-ZO

4 Schindler House

Map U, P.107

The pinnacle of California living, this under-statedly iconic house was conceived by the Austrian architect R.M. Schindler (1887–1953) and his American wife Pauline (1893–1977) in 1921. Now serving as the MAK Center for Art and Architecture, L.A., the house sits on a residential street in West Hollywood. Inspired by the temperate climate, the residence and immaculate gardens integrate open air sleeping porches and outdoor fireplaces. The house, open to the public from Wednesday through Saturday, embodies one of the first examples of true indoor/outdoor living.

© MAK Center. Photo by Gerald Zugman.

© MAK Center. Photo by Joshua White.

🕐 1100–1800 (W–Su)   💲 $7/6
🏠 835 North Kings Rd., CA 90069
📞 +1 (323) 651 1510   🔗 www.makcenter.org
✐ Free admission: 1600–1800 (F)

"The Schindler house marks a jumping-off point into the exploration of the innovative and ever-evolving design climate of Los Angeles."
– Thom Mayne, Morphsis Architect

5 Eames House

Map AC, P.108

© Eames Office, LLC

The iconic home of Ray (1912–88) and Charles Eames (1907–78) represents the pinnacle of the mid-century modernist movement in California. Part of the Case Study House Program, the colorful and playful home acted as the primary residence of the design power couple. The prefabricated house demonstrates how work, play, life, and nature can peacefully coexist. Group visits can be arranged for the exterior only while guided tours of the lower floor are available for 1–4 guests at a time. There are no restrooms on site so be sure to plan in advance.

🕙 1000–1600 (M–Tu, Th–Sa)
🏠 203 Chautauqua Blvd., CA 90272
📞 +1 (310) 459 9663
URL www.eamesfoundation.org
🎟 *Exterior self-guided tours: $10. 1 hour interior tours: $450, for 3–4 adults. Both required reservations.*

© Eames Office, LLC

"While you can't go inside, the giant windows give you a glimpse through time into the world of the genius couple."

– Patrick Hruby

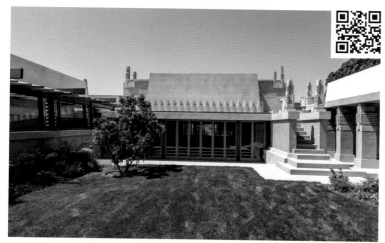

6 Hollyhock House
Map E, P.100

An architecture tour of Los Angeles feels incomplete without a visit to a Frank Lloyd Wright house. Perched on a hill, this impressive bunker-like residence was built for an oil heiress in 1921. Due to Wright's (1867–1959) commitments with other projects, much of the residence was completed by his assistant Rudolph Schindler (1887–1953). This unusual hybrid between two great architectural minds features an abstracted hollyhock pattern that wraps the exterior. Bring a picnic and enjoy sweeping views of the city.

🏠 Barnsdall Park, 4800 Hollywood Blvd.,
CA 90027 📞 +1 (323) 913 4031
🌐 www.barnsdall.org/visit/hollyhock-house
🔗 "Walk Wright In" self-guided tours: 1100–1600
(Th–Su). Last entry at 1515, $7/3

"Frank Lloyd Wright's iconographic architecture is a must see. Its location is also beautiful at Barnsdall Park with a museum to check out as well."
– Shark Toof

7 Bradbury Building
Map M, P.104

Since 1893, a piece of cinematic and architectural history continues to stand on a main corner of Downtown Los Angeles. The landmark building wraps levels of offices around a soaring Victorian atrium filled with light. While the public cannot go beyond the ground floor, it remains worth dropping by to marvel at the original and ornate cast iron work, expressive elevator system, and glass ceilings. While a bit antiquated now, the technology integrated here catapulted Los Angeles into the twentieth century.

🕑 0900–1800 (M–F), –1700 (Sa–Su)
🏠 304 S. Broadway, CA 90013   📞 +1 (213) 626 1893

"It's the oldest commercial space in LA, and to me has specific, cultural significance as it was used in the movie, Blade Runner."

– Neil Huxley

8 Al Struckus House
Map AF, P.109

A forgotten gem designed by legendary architect Bruce Goff (1904–82) perches on a wooded hill overlooking the San Fernando Valley. Glass tiles and undulating stucco accent the redwood cladding. Four domed windows give the home an alien and futuristic quality. Completed in 1984 for Al Struckus – an engineer, woodworker, and art collector who detailed much of the house himself – the eccentric cylindrical home remains closed except for occasional private tours. Drive by anyway and marvel at the whimsical structure from the street.

🏠 4510 Saltillo St., CA 91364

"One of the weirdest private homes in the US and a great example of Organic Architecture!"

– Ben Mor

9 Cinerama Dome
Map F, P.101

This Hollywood landmark, first opened in 1963, continues to welcome film buffs into its iconic domed interior. Now home to ArcLight Cinemas, the regal theater provides reserved seating so book ahead of time for the best spot. Unlike most theaters in the city, the ArcLight caters to a more adult crowd with a full open bar perfect for date night. Don't be fooled by the retro appearance, this theater features the latest technologies for a world-class cinematic experience.

🕐 Café: 1130–0000 daily
💲 Ticket price varies with programs
📍 6360 W. Sunset Blvd., CA 90028
📞 +1 (323) 464 1478
URL www.arclightcinemas.com

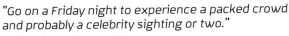

"Go on a Friday night to experience a packed crowd and probably a celebrity sighting or two."

– Bobby Solomon, The Fox Is Black

Los Angeles River
Map A, P.99

The concrete paradise of the Los Angeles River cuts across 48 miles of Southern California. In parts a mysterious graffiti-covered wasteland and in others a lush bioregion for wildlife, the river prevents flooding during the rainy season. With extensive revitalization plans in the works, the time to visit the river in its full idiosyncratic glory is now. Begin at the 1920s Hyperion Bridge and spend the day picnicking and hiking through the basin backed by the tranquil sounds of water lapping, cranes taking flight, and distant passing cars.

URL www.lariver.org, folar.org
Restrooms & wifi available at The Frog Spot (2825 Benedict St., LA 90039): 0800–1600 (Sa–Su)

"Forget what you think about the L.A. River. Try a night visit with someone special, entering through the gate of Los Feliz Boulevard."

– Gina Clyne

11 Ennis House
Map D, P.100

Situated in the hills of Los Feliz, this futuristic dwelling by Frank Lloyd Wright (1867–1959) can be seen from his Hollyhock House (#6), just a hill to the south. The 1920s house incorporates a Mayan-influenced cladding of 27,000 orna-mental concrete blocks and a tempting pool overlooking the city. Hollywood productions from *Blade Runner (1982)* to a Michael Jackson video have captured this timeless house on film. Easily visible but currently closed to the public, the house just found a new owner after two years on the market.

🏠 *2607 Glendower Ave., CA 90027*
URL *ennishouse.com*

"The house is a true masterpiece and a must see."
– Danny Boy O'Connor, House of Pain & La Coka Nostra

12 Chateau Marmont

Map Y, P.108

A Hollywood institution continues to serve as the tantalizing backdrop for the rich and famous. The glamorous hotel, restaurant, and bar have remained the ultimate celebrity destination since its opening in 1927. Whether turning away Lindsay Lohan or welcoming in the likes of F. Scott Fitzgerald and Sofia Coppola, the chateau acts as a creative and social muse for the city. Nestled behind dense hedges on Sunset Boulevard, the chateau keeps its legend alive with first rate cuisine and cocktails.

🏠 *8221 Sunset Blvd., CA 90046*
📞 *+1 (323) 656 1010*
URL *www.chateaumarmont.com*

"You can drive by the Hollywood sign or walk a block of the stars on Hollywood, but dinner and drinks at the Chateau gets you inside a piece of Hollywood history."

– Rich Sommer

Cultural & Art Spaces

Contemporary art, experimental projects, and thematic movie theaters

Cheaper rents, plentiful sunshine, and a contagious "can-do" attitude make the city one of the global hotspots for culture and art. Museums both large and small supported by a vibrant gallery scene host innovative exhibitions from emerging and established artists. The centrally located Los Angeles County Museum of Art (#17), the west side's Getty Center (#13), and the Getty Villa (*www.getty.edu*) in Malibu each deserve a day visit to appreciate their expansive collections from antiquity to the contemporary. For a more off the beaten path experience, the endlessly idiosyncratic Museum of Jurassic Technology in Palms (#20) and Machine Project (#18) – the nucleus of irreverent happenings – in Echo Park curate memorable showcases entrenched in irony and whimsy. The Museum of Contemporary Art's downtown locations (#14) can be paired with gallery visits. Check out the Chinatown galleries clustered along the scenic Chung King Road or the experimental east side Night Gallery (*nightgallery.ca*) and 356 Mission (#22). Keep an eye on the Hammer's (#15), Cinespia's (*cinespia.org*), and the Cinefamily's (#24) countless film screenings, artist talks, and more. The abundance of art shows and cultural events will easily surpass the number of days of your trip so make sure to start researching ahead of time.

Hrishikesh Hirway
Musician & graphic designer

I make my records under moniker The One AM Radio, score films, and produce a podcast called Song Exploder. I love this city, its culture, and its constant sunshine.

The Getty Center P.032

MOCA P.034

Aleks Kocev
Photographer

I'm a commercial photographer specializing in lifestyle and landscape work. When I'm not enjoying my hometown and my dogs I'm off on the road.

Poketo
Lifestyle store

Ted Vadakan and Angie Myung co-founded Poketo in 2003. Devoted to bringing art and design to everyday life, Poketo has been growing from a creative enterprise to a lifestyle brand.

Hammer Museum P.035

Justin Harder
Graphic designer

With over ten years in the commercial and entertainment field, and also experience in illustrations, copywriting, and creative direction. I also manage production studio Claus.

Art Center College of Design P.036

LACMA P.038

Misty Lee
Magician & actress

Am honored to be the first female 'Ghost Host' of the Houdini Séance show at the Magic Castle in Hollywood, and am thrilled to be showing you around my town!

Gai Gherardi
Co-founder, l.a.Eyeworks

Barbara McReynolds and I design adventurous, vibrant frames that celebrate the diversity of faces and provoke the uniqueness of individuals.

Machine Project P.040

Leland Jackson
Visual & sound artist

Most known for my experimental sonic work under the alias Ahnnu, I produce music that reflects a wealth of genres and tastes from hip hop to electroacoustic compositions.

The Museum of Jurassic Technology
P.042

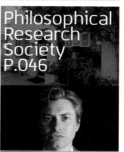

Paige Smith
Street artist

Also known as A Common Name, I create dimensional "urban geode" installations that explode out of walls and cracks in the city. My work is a piece of beauty in the mundane.

Nico Stai
Musician

I am a musician, singer, writer of songs and chaser of tones based in Silver Lake, Echo Park and Downtown LA.

Space 15 Twenty
P.041

The Wiltern
P.044

Jimmy Marble
Director & photographer

I am a director and photographer. My work is extremely colorful and often humorous but without jokes.

Philosophical Research Society
P.046

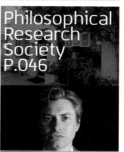

Shane Hutton
Co-founder, Arcana Academy

I'm a creative director and I've been fortunate enough to win the Grand Prix at Cannes, be nominated for an Emmy, and have my work appear in over 35 museums worldwide.

Tim Nackashi
Film & video director

From Florida, I'm probably most known for my music videos for OK Go, Neon Indian, TV On The Radio and others in addition to my documentary Dirty Work, a Sundance official selection.

356 Mission
P.045

The Cinefamily
P.047

031

13 The Getty Center
Map X, P.108

This hilltop museum designed by Richard Meier opened its doors in 1997. Once the world's most expensive building, the $1.3 billion project features 16,000 tons of Italian travertine. The museum offers permanent and rotating exhibitions of European and American artworks from medieval times to today. Reached by tram, the immaculate grounds culminate with Robert Irwin's tranquil Central Gardens. On a clear day, one can take in the full panorama of Los Angeles from downtown to the Pacific Ocean.

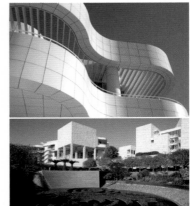

- ⏰ 1000–1730 (Tu–F, Su), –2100 (Su)
- 🏠 1200 N. Sepulveda Blvd., CA 90049
- ☎ +1 (310) 440 7300
- URL www.getty.edu

"Spend the day just roaming the buildings and gardens of the Getty. The Center itself acts as Starfleet Academy in the JJ Abrams Star Trek films."
– Hrishikesh Hirway

14 MOCA

Map K, P.102, Map M & N, P.104

With two main venues downtown (DT) and a smaller annex at the Pacific Design Center (PDC), the Museum of Contemporary Art presents innovative and thought provoking exhibitions. The museum boasts one of the countries most extensive contemporary art collections with over 6,800 pieces spanning from 1940 through today. The Geffen Contemporary, the museum's second downtown location, hosts Printed Matter's annual LA Art Book Fair each January. Since 1979, MOCA's stunning art collection, ambitious lectures, and education programs continue to attract loyal visitors.

🕐 DT: 1100–1700 (M & F), –2000 (Th), –1800 (Sa–Su), PDC: 1100–1700 (Tu–F), –1800 (Sa–Su) 💲 DT: $12/7 🏠 DT: 250 S. Grand Ave. / 152 N. Central Ave., CA 90012, PDC: 8687 Melrose Ave., CA 90069 🔗 moca.org 📎 Free admittance (DT): 1700–2000 (Th)

"I'm never disappointed and most often inspired by the work I see there. Stop by the gift shop and bring some culture back with you."

– Aleks Kocev

15 Hammer Museum
Map Z, P.108

Set in the heart of Westwood Village, this museum acts as one of the best venues for viewing contemporary art in the city. Thanks to a generous endowment received earlier in 2014, the museum is now free to the public. The multiple galleries wind around a shady central courtyard, perfect for taking a break between exhibitions. Film screenings, concerts, workshops, and artist talks keep the museum at the forefront of cultural and artistic taste making.

🕐 1100–2000 (Tu–F), –1700 (Sa–Su)
📍 10899 Wilshire Blvd., CA 90024
📞 +1 (310) 443 7000
URL hammer.ucla.edu

"The Hammer stands apart from other museums thanks to its commitment to original curation. The courtyard is a great place to linger over a book with a coffee."

– Angie Myung & Ted Vadakan, Poketo

16 Art Center College of Design

Map AD, P.109

Designed by the California modernist Craig
Ellwood (1922–92), this piece of architectural
history also serves as the home for one of
the state's most cutting edge art schools. The
striking building functions as a bridge, hover-
ing over the main roadway in a wooded patch
of Pasadena. A curated gallery showcases the
best from the school's body of film, product
design, and visual art students. Spend a day enjoying the work, sculpture garden, and tranquil
grounds but make sure to watch out for the
occasional rattle snake!

🏠 1700 Lida St., CA 91103
URL www.artcenter.edu

*"There's a brilliant view which gives you a sense of
peace and serenity while you are there. On top of that
I went there so there's school pride!"*
– Justin Harder

17 LACMA
Map O, P.104

The largest museum in the Western United States, Los Angeles County Museum of Art's Miracle Mile location features a collection of over 120,000 objects from antiquity to the present day. The newly opened Broad Art Center by Renzo Piano rounds off the contemporary art wing while Chris Burden's Urban Light installation, Michael Heizer's Levitated Mass, and glimpses of the La Brea Tar Pits can be enjoyed free of charge in the outdoor spaces. Enjoy exhibitions by legendary and local artists and then grab a burger at Ray & Starks Bar.

🕐 1100–1700 (M–Tu, Th), –2000 (F), 1000–1900 (Sa–Su)
💲 $15/10, Specially ticketed exhibitions: $25
🏠 5905 Wilshire Blvd., CA 90036
📞 +1 (323) 857 6000 URL www.lacma.org

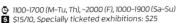

"The iconic, solar-powered "Urban Light" exhibit outside is one of my favorite sites in all of LA."
– Misty Lee

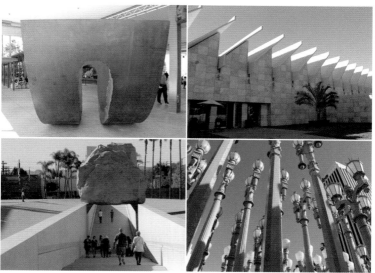

18 Machine Project
Map G, P.101

A tiny storefront in Echo Park hosts some of
the most innovative and experimental art projects in LA. The brainchild of the tireless Mark
Allen, the space offers an eccentric and changing mix of installations, poetry readings, plays,
jam making sessions, and much more. Sign up
for the mailing list to find out what's in store
for the week. From sea shanty sing-alongs
to avant-garde performances in the recently
opened underground mini-theater, the happenings at Machine Project consistently defy
expectations.

🕐 Opening time varies with
program (usually at 2000)
🏠 1200-D N. Alvarado St., CA 90026
📞 +1 (213) 483 8761
URL machineproject.com

"*Imagine a place where no idea is too outlandish to
be taken seriously, and there you have
Machine Project.*"
– Gai Gherardi, l.a.Eyeworks

19 Space 15 Twenty
Map F, P.101

An intimate courtyard of connected retailers hides behind prominent red brick walls. The inspiring setting attracts the usual and unusual to this Hollywood hotspot. Since 2009, the commercial hub hosts small creative shops, pop up events, craft nights, film screenings, live music, and more. Make sure to give yourself enough time to peruse this location of Hennessey + Ingalls, the largest art book store in the Western United States.

🕐 1000–2200 (M-Sa), –2100 (Su), Hennessey + Ingalls: 1100–2000 (M-F), 1000– (Sa-Su)
🏠 1520 N. Cahuenga Blvd., CA 90028
URL www.space15twenty.com

"Check out Hennessy + Ingalls for a nice read and swing by next door for a crazy delicious burger from Umami Burger. Trust me."

– Leland Jackson aka Ahnnu

20 The Museum of Jurassic Technology
Map AA, P.108

A nondescript storefront on Venice Boulevard hides the ultimate cabinet of curiosity just inside. The tiny oddities museum exhibits a fantastical hybrid of fact and fiction ranging from micro sculptures of Pope John Paul II and Napoleon that fit in the eye of a needle to a shrine to the brave dogs of the Soviet Space Program. The top floor Tula Tea Room serves complimentary tea and cookies while the Borzoi Kabinet Theater screens a film each hour.

🕐 1400–2000 (Th), 1200–1800 (F–Su)
💲 $8/5 🏠 9341 Venice Blvd., CA 90232 📞 +1 (310) 836 6131
URL www.mjt.org

"This is a great space to spend a Sunday afternoon. I don't want to give too much away, I just highly recommend it."

– Paige Smith aka A Common Name

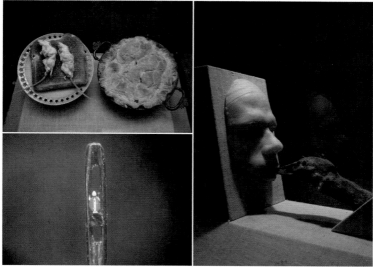

21 The Wiltern
Map R, P.106

Originally opened as the Warner Brothers Western Theater, the elegant emerald colored venue hosts live concerts by local and world famous musicians. Whether coming for the music, architecture, or both, the Wiltern is not to be missed. The theater, now standing room only, accommodates up to 1,400 people per show. Make sure to arrive early to marvel at the star burst ceiling and exuberant Art Deco ornament bursting out of every corner. They really don't make 'em like they used to.

🏠 3790 Wilshire Blvd., CA 90010
☎ +1 (213) 388 1400
URL www.wiltern.com

"An amazing art deco building from an era when things were made to be beautiful, both inside and out."
– Nico Stai

22 356 Mission
Map Q, P.105

Operated by the same owners of the bookstore/boutique Ooga Booga in Chinatown LA, this new gallery space in Boyle Heights builds upon the institution's curatorial skills. The gallery and event space hosts a range of inspired and of the moment exhibitions and art events in a large, repurposed industrial building. From book launches to avant-garde performances and artist talks, the multi-purpose creative hotspot is the place to go to learn about the emerging stars of the LA art scene.

🕐 1100–1800 (W–Su)
🏠 356 S. Mission Rd., CA 90033, Ooga Booga
Chinatown: #203 943 N. Broadway, CA 90012
📞 +1 (323) 609 3162 🔳 356mission.com

"365 Mission is a new and amazingly curated gallery in a giant and inspiring space on the east side."

– Jimmy Marble

23 Philosophical Research Society

Map A, P.98

Founded in 1934, this treasure trove of philo-
sophical literature resides in an unpretentious
storefront in Los Feliz. The organization acts
as an invaluable resource for the study and
research of philosophy. Encompassing an
extensive library, bookstore, and publishing
house, the institution provides a safe haven
for scholarly study and shared discourse. The
library, open to the public, hosts an extremely
valuable collection of rare and out of print
editions. As such, all books must be enjoyed on
the premises.

🕙 1000–1600 (M–F)
🏠 3910 Los Feliz Blvd., CA 90027
📞 +1 (800) 548 4062
URL www.prs.org

*"Founded by noted philosopher and scholar Manly P.
Hall, this place houses one of the largest and rarest
collections of esoteric books in the world."*
– Shane Hutton, Arcana Academy

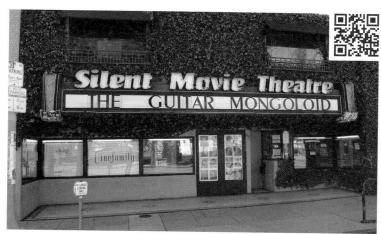

24 The Cinefamily
Map L, P.103

A former silent movie theater now presents one of the most eclectic film programs in town. Founded in 2007 by the Harkham brothers and Hadrian Belove, founder of Cinefile Video, the ivy-covered non-profit stages a social atmosphere as an integral part of the movie-going experience. With an average of 14 screenings per week and something for every taste, the intimate theater's offerings also feature special guests, live music, dance parties, the occasional potluck, and director talks. The cinema includes an intimate courtyard out back where guests are often invited to enjoy complimentary beers and hot dogs.

🕐 Box office: 1 hour before first show to 30 mins after the start of last show daily
💲 Ticket price varies with programs
🏠 611 N. Fairfax Ave., CA 90036
📞 +1 (323) 655 2510 URL www.cinefamily.org

"This is an incredible film venue to see nearly forgotten avant-garde films, restored masterpieces, pure schlock, silent films and many more!"

– Tim Nackashi

Markets & Shops

Curated music records, vintage gear, and mixed literature

A shopper's paradise, Los Angeles has something for everyone provided you know where to look. Skip the malls and the overpriced tourist trap of Rodeo Drive and head to one of the city's main shopping districts. Practice some retail therapy in Venice on the boutique-packed Abbot Kinney strip. Highlights include a visit to Tortoise General Supply (#29) and their gallery space out back for an infusion of Japanese goods and culture. While not quite as endearingly grungy as it used to be, Melrose Avenue (#25) still offers a trove of quirky and more upscale retail options. Vermont Avenue in the heart of Los Feliz stands as yet another gold mine for vintage finds, the latest international designs, and fresh literary releases from the always charming Skylight Books (#33). Music lovers should be sure not miss Old Style Guitars (#32), Freakbeat Records (#34), and Mount Analog (#26) sprinkled across the east side and valley. Finish off your shopping spree and do some good at the Time Travel Mart (#35) in Echo Park. Founded by Dave Eggers, this quirky storefront has everything to meet your esoteric time travel needs. Proceeds go toward teaching school children how to write in the tutoring facility behind the shop.

Plastic Jesus
Street artist

Plastic Jesus specializes in bold stencil and installation work. He combines humor and criticism, inspired by world news, the society, the urban environment, culture and politics.

Melrose
Avenue
P.052

Mount Analog
P.053

Rob Carmichael
Founder, SEEN

Carmichael starts and ends every day by kissing his wife, his two children and feeding the cat. In the middle of somewhere, he makes graphic design for a number of good folks.

Hassan Rahim
Artist & art director

I'm an artist and art director from Los Angeles, exhibiting my personal works internationally and working on client projects within the music and fashion industries.

Mohawk
General
Store
P.054

69
Denim label

69 wishes to provide everyone with a chill lifestyle in denim. We want to help you be comfortable.

69
Showroom
P.055

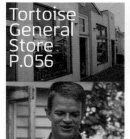

Tortoise
General
Store
P.056

Kivi Sotamaa
Architect

I'm an architect, designer, thinker and pioneer of digital design technology based in Helsinki and LA. I'm also the founder of ADD Aalto University Digital Design Laboratory.

Iris Anna Regn
Architect

With a multi-disciplinary social practice, my work ranges in scale, from the design of buildings, interiors, and products, to curating, programing, and designing exhibitions.

California
Millinery Supply
Company
P.057

Hugh Kretschmer
Photographer

I am a father, photographer, director, educator, craftsman, collaborator, and late bloomer. In my work, human nature is illustrated through quirk and irony.

Old Style Guitar Shop P.059

Bo Mirosseni
Filmmaker

A native of Los Angeles, I got my start doing skate videos and from there gradually progressed into specializing in music videos and commercials.

Joel Arquillos
Executive director, 826LA

Joel is a proud husband, father and occasional musician. He directs 826LA, which is a non-profit writing and tutoring center that serves the young.

The Original Farmers Market P.058

Skylight Books P.060

Time Travel Mart P.062

Darren Weiss
Artist, writer & musician, PAPA

Born and raised in LA, I work as an artist, writer, and musician in the band PAPA. I grew up in Encino and have lived in Echo Park for several years.

Alexa Meade
Artist

After nomadically travelling for three years, Alexa fell in love with LA and called it her home in 2013. Her style of optical illusion makes a 3D space look deceptively like a 2D oil painting.

Steven Harrington
Artist & designer

His bright and iconic style encourages a two-way conversation between viewers and the artist. He co-founded design agency National Forest and pop-art brand You&I.

Freakbeat Records P.061

St. Vincent de Paul Store P.063

25 Melrose Avenue
Map L, P.103

This once seedy street now stands as one of the city's chic shopping areas. First made famous by the television series Melrose Place, this long shopping strip packs in a variety of vintage clothing shops, increasingly upscale boutiques, cafés, restaurants, and bars. Spend the afternoon searching for retro treasures in Wasteland, American Vintage, and Resurrection or people watch from one of the many bustling brunch spots. Still a mecca for local street art, Melrose retains much of its authentic charm.

URL *Resurrection: www. resurrectionvintage.com, Sunday flea market: melrosetradingpost.org, Lucques: www.lucques.com*

"Don't go early as no one who shops on Melrose wakes up before midday."
– Plastic Jesus

26 Mount Analog
Map C, P.99

This impeccably curated independent music shop attracts a high caliber crowd of record collectors and creative enthusiasts. Conveniently located at the Highland Park (Gold Line) Station, the retail space doubles as a record shop, clothing boutique, art gallery, event space, bookstore, and more. The space features an adventurous collection of cutting edge music, art, literature, and fashion. A community hub where artist and audience come together, the shop hosts a variety of exhibitions, readings, book signings, and performances.

🕐 1200–2000 (Tu–Sa), –1800 (Su)
🏠 5906 1/2 N. Figueroa St., CA 90042
📞 +1 (323) 474 6649
URL climbmountanalog.com

"If you are a record collector then you've already hit up Amoeba, but Mount Analog is a total gem dedicated to out-there sounds of all stripes."

– Rob Carmichael, SEEN

27 **Mohawk General Store**
Map H, P.101

Owned by Bo and Kevin Carney, Mohawk
General Store began when the stylish couple
decided to share their passion for fashion with
the public. Bo's style merges baggy, simple, chic,
casual, and feminine aesthetics into a distinctive look while Kevin embraces a more mascu-
line sensibility. More than just clothing stores, all
three Mohawk locations showcase one of a kind
housewares from high quality candles, lights,
and dishes to flasks and decorative sculptures.
The two stores in Silver Lake cater to women's
and menswear while the Pasadena location
stocks exclusively women's gear.

🕐 1100–1900 (M–Sa), –1800 (Su) 🏠 4011 & 4017 W.
Sunset Blvd., CA 90029 📞 +1 (323) 669 1601
🔗 www.mohawkgeneralstore.com

"*A blend between luxury items and casual daily
wearable goods. Also selling vintage audio and some
furniture. LA's best.*"
– Hassan Rahim

28 69 Showroom

Map P, P.104

Made in the present but intended for the future, the elusive design company 69 has a top secret showroom for testing out their latest clothing and products. The brand maintains a timeless yet contemporary mystique with its loose fitting and unisex denim, linen, and cotton styles. While insisting on complete anonymity, the company headquarters are open to the public by appointment only. Set up your exclusive shopping experience through email.

🏠 #810, Fashion Bldg., 120 E. 8th St, CA 90014 **URL** www.sixty-nine.us
🔗 By appointment only via whatsup@sixty-nine.us

"Shop therapy at its finest in the real world."

– 69

29 Tortoise General Store
Map W, P.107

A small store on Abbot Kinney presents a refined selection of Japanese products. The tasteful items, made from high quality materials, adhere to a strict aesthetic and pragmatic agenda. Seamlessly blending art, craft, and design, the Japanese importer and retailer specializes in modern housewares, gifts, and furniture. After shopping, make sure to pay a visit to the *TORTOISE gallery space just behind the store. This gallery exhibits an intriguing group of Japanese artists that work with traditional Japanese handcraft techniques.

🕐 1000–1800 (M–Sa), 1200–(Su)
🏠 1208 Abbot Kinney Blvd., CA 90291
☎ +1 (310) 314 8448
URL tortoisegeneralstore.com

"Most of the things at Tortoise you can imagine owning and living with for years."

– Kivi Sotamaa

30 California Millinery Supply Company
Map P, P.104

True to its name, this obscure shop caters to your every need related to women's hats. The densely packed store offers a treasure trove of millinery supplies from hat making tools to wig and toupee bases and frames. A museum-like time capsule of a bygone era of fashion, the shop has changed little since the 1940s. Wander the antiquated aisles stacked high with feathers, hand-woven Mexican raffia flowers, and miniature paper mâché fruit to design the hat of your dreams.

🕐 0900-1730 (M-F), 1300-1600 (Sa)
🏠 721 S. Spring St., CA 90014
📞 +1 (213) 622 8746
URL www.californiamillinery.net

"I can't imagine this place still existing in another city – it's one of the positive side effects of the former demise of Downtown Los Angeles."

– Iris Anna Regn

31 The Original Farmers Market
Map L, P.103

First opened in 1934, the classic open-air market exudes a vintage charm that only comes with time. The packed stalls present a range of international family-run food stalls, gift shops, traditional and artisanal bakeries, and even a butcher. Simple café tables sprinkled throughout allow guests to dine and people watch in the thick of the action. For a mix of retro and contemporary experiences, take your frozen chocolate covered banana on a short walk to the popular mecca of kitsch shopping – the Grove.

🕘 0900–2100 (M-F), –2000 (Sa), 1000–1900 (Su)
🏠 6333 W. 3rd St., CA 90036
📞 +1 (323) 933 9211
URL www.farmersmarketla.com

"I recommend stopping by Kip's Toyland, Magic Nut and Candy Company, and Pampas Brazilian Grill."

– Hugh Kretschmer

32 Old Style Guitar Shop
Map AH, P.109

Just south of Sunset Boulevard, an old wooden house doubles as one of the music industry's go-to places for rare, restored, and unusual instruments and equipment. The living room turned showroom attracts the audiophile and layman alike. Intimate and quirky, the boutique guitar shop features an unusual selection of antique and vintage instruments that extend far beyond guitars and bases. Beckoning to the music lover in us all, this surprising shop fluctuates between place of business and cave of wonders.

- ⏰ 1300–1800 (Tu–Sa), –1700 (Su)
- 🏠 510 A N. Hoover St., CA 90004
- 📞 +1 (323) 660 5700
- 🔗 oldstyleguitarshop.com

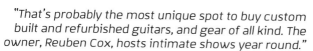

"That's probably the most unique spot to buy custom built and refurbished guitars, and gear of all kind. The owner, Reuben Cox, hosts intimate shows year round."

– Joel Arquillos, 826LA

33 **Skylight Books**
Map E, P.100

One of the last independent bookstores in Los Angeles resides in the bustling shopping district of Los Feliz village. Catering to a sub-culture market true to its neighborhood, the spacious bookshop contains an extensive collection of contemporary fiction, art, and photography books as well as more underground graphic novels and comic books. A perfect place to spend an afternoon or evening, the shop – open daily until 10pm – hosts a variety of readings and signings by outstanding artists and authors.

⏱ 1000–2200 daily
🏠 1818 N. Vermont Ave., CA 90027
📞 +1 (323) 660 1175 URL www.skylightbooks.com

"I can spend hours in this place. It's awesome a local bookstore like this is still in business so you should support them when you find some time."

– Bo Mirosseni

34 Freakbeat Records
Map AG, P.109

This curated music haven stands as one of the last independent record stores in Southern California. The store brings customers back to the days where shopping for music was fun and adventurous. New and used vinyl fill up half the store. Browse through collectible records or dig through the 99 cent room for bargain buys. Never mind the valley location and pared down selection, the neighborhood record store may not have everything you want but will always have something you need.

🕐 1100–2000 (M-Sa), 1200–1800 (Su)
🏠 13616 Ventura Blvd., CA 91423
📞 +1 (818) 995 7603 URL freakbeatrecords.com

"The two owners (who work at the cash register) know more about music than anybody I know, and they aren't afraid to share their knowledge."

– Darren Weiss, PAPA

35 Time Travel Mart
Map G, P.101

"Whenever you are, we are already then" is the motto of this whimsical concept store. The brainchild of Dave Eggers, the playful shop supports the nonprofit writing and tutoring center 826LA. The tutoring facility, nestled behind the jars of robot milk, provides after school support to students aged 6–18. Grab a dinosaur egg, some communist soap for your favorite eccentric friend or a "Future Human" onesie for your baby. Proceeds of your timeless purchase help teach kids to write.

**Fresh!
DINOSAUR
EGGS**
Large $9.99 Small $4.99
Please do not slam refrigerator door, premie dinos require extra special care.

🕐 1200–1800 daily   🏠 Echo Park: 1714 Sunset Blvd., CA 90026, Mar Vista: 12515 Venice Blvd., CA 90066

URL www.timetravelmart.com

"Your go-to place for satisfying your time travel related needs such as '5 More Minutes on Your Expired Parking Meter'."
– Alexa Meade

36 St. Vincent de Paul Store
Map S, P.106

Named after the great French Saint known for his exceptional generosity to the poor, this thrift shop is not just a store it's a community. Built on a shared love of helping for the greater good, the massive warehouse space serves as a treasure trove for those who enjoy the hunt. While this second hand location may not fit into your usual vintage shopping circuit, its massive inventory guarantees that they will have almost everything you're looking or didn't know you were looking for. From books to large furniture and even cars, an afternoon spent at St. Vincent's is sure to turn up some unexpected gems.

🕒 *0930–1800 (M–Sa), 0900–1700 (Su)*
📍 *210 N. Ave. 21, CA 90031*
📞 *+1 (323) 224 6280* **URL** *www.svdpla.org*

"Books and books and books, furniture, art, and most of all inspiration is delivered daily. If you're not afraid to visit thrift stores, then this is an absolute must!"

– Steven Harrington

Restaurants & Cafés

Skillful American classics, Italian fare, tacos, and spicy Asian delights

The best thing to bring on your trip to Los Angeles is an empty stomach. First rate culinary options from across the globe are represented by the city's flourishing Korean, Japanese, Chinese, Thai, Armenian, and Ethiopian populations (just to name a few). For regional specialities from the budget to the boutique, Los Angeles offers a spectrum of satisfying options and an abundance of star chefs including Wolfgang Punk and Mario Batali. No visit to LA feels complete without indulging in some Mexican food so be sure to grab an authentic and affordable bite from one of the city's numerous taco trucks or the famed hole in the wall, El Tapatio (#43). Those seeking more culinary adventure should make a reservation at Animal (#45), where any part of the animal can and will end up on your plate. Speranza (#48), Bestia (#38), and Gjelina offer Italian influenced cuisine and lively atmospheres, and pop-up restaurant LASA serves up high quality Filipino cuisine (www.lasarestaurant.com) once in a while. To dine with a view of the ocean, visit the organic seasonal Malibu Farm (#37) on the scenic Pacific Coast Highway. Compliment one of your meals with a visit to the quaint Kaldi Coffee (#44) to experience the city's cold press coffee phenomenon first hand.

PJ Richardson
Co-founder, Laundry!

From LA, we create design, animation and visual effects – storytelling with a twist.

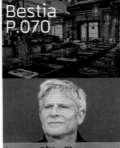

Bestia
P.070

Heather McGinn
Partner, ALLTHATISSOLID

Influenced by design-rich LA, the wealth of science and graphic industries in the city, my work pursues a collaborative rapport with adjacent disciplines.

Lorcan O'Herlihy
Founder & principal, LOHA

Born in Dublin, raised in LA, the architect seeks to engage the ever changing urban landscape. LOHA has been recognized by 75 awards, including the 2010 AIA LA Firm of the Year Award.

Malibu Farm
P.068

Gracias Madre
P.072

Eve Speciall
DJ, model & music director

I'm a Sydney born, LA-based DJ, music director by way of Hong Kong, celiac, purveyor of the perfect poached egg, avid skier, mother to fat french bulldog/boston terrier Butters.

Night + Market Song
P.074

Nite Jewel
Musician

California native Ramona Gonzalez develops her minimalist dance-pop escapades and has released albums Good Evening and One Second of Love under the moniker Nite Jewel.

Sean Pecknold
Filmmaker

I am a filmmaker and stop-motion animator from Seattle Washington. I like riding my bike on the LA river.

POT
@The Line
P.073

Town Pizza
P.075

De Lux
Musicians

We are Isaac Franco and Sean Guerin. We write music as De Lux and play golf at night when the ranges close.

Kaldi Coffee
P.077

Kirsten Lepore
Director & animator

A MFA graduate from CalArts, I've done client work for MTV, Google, Facebook, and my films have gone around the world. I'm a fan of silly dance moves, subwoofers and weird foods.

Molly Cranna
Photographer

I live in Silver Lake and specialize in editorial and commercial portraiture and still life work. In my spare time, I study maps of NE LA and explore strange Canadian suburbs on Google street view.

Taqueria
El Tapatio
P.076

Animal
Restaurant
P.078

Dustin Edward Arnold
Creative director

Dustin is a transmedia creative director with a background in spatial design, emerging media and photography. His clients include Issey Miyake, Nike Japan and Alexandre Plokhov.

El
Huarachito
P.080

Benjamin Ball
Set designer

Benjamin Ball explores the intersection of architecture, art and product design. His work include films, music videos and commercials, as well as Disney Concert Hall and event design.

Barbara Bestor
Principal, Bestor Architecture

Founding chair of the graduate program at Woodbury University's School of Architecture and author of Bohemian Modern, Living in Silver Lake (Harper Collins, 2006).

Edendale
P.079

Speranza
P.081

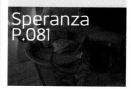

37 Malibu Farm
Map AB, P.108

Right on the Malibu Pier, a quaint café provides the perfect stopping point for admiring the Pacific over an organic and understated meal. The restaurant, which first began its operations out of the owner's backyard, now serves daily meals with the finest local ingredients. With many items harvested from the owner's personal gardens, the simply prepared dishes accent the impressive coastline. Whether seated inside or out, unobstructed ocean panoramas make this restaurant a destination in its own right.

🕐 0900-1530 (M-Tu), -2030 (W-Th, Su), -2100 (F-Sa) 🏠 23000 Pacific Coast Hwy, CA 90265
📞 +1 (310) 456 1112
URL www.malibu-farm.com
🔗 Dinner reservations start at 1630

"On a nice day, it's beautiful to walk out, stop at the coo little surf shop and try for some breakfast or lunch at th café. Ask for quinoa oatmeal or the cauliflower pizza."
– PJ Richardson, Laundry!

38 Bestia
Map Q, P.105

Tucked away in a dead end alley in Downtown's Arts District, this Italian restaurant never disappoints. The restaurant, led by a young husband and wife duo, serves up some of the freshest pastas and pizzas in town. Over 60 varieties of charcuterie, homemade gelato, and pizzas cooked in a wood burning stove represent just a few of the tantalizing options awaiting patrons. The industrial feeling of the restaurant paired with the inviting menu make this a mom and pop restaurant to remember.

🕐 1700-2300 (Su-Th), -0000 (F-Sa)
🏠 2121 7th Pl., CA 90021
📞 +1 (213) 514 5724 🔗 bestiala.com

"The pasta and pizzas are magnificent – the experience mixes the gritty industrial feel of downtown's edge with trendy fine dining."

– Lorcan O'Herlihy, LOHA

39 Gracias Madre
Map K, P.102

Located on a chic strip of Melrose Avenue, this organic vegan Mexican restaurant stands as the second culinary brainchild of the owners of the immensely popular, and equally worth a visit, Café Gratitude. The plant-based cuisine, paired with impeccably curated cocktails, features locally grown produce and homegrown corn varieties. The seasonal offerings and understated atmosphere make it the perfect restaurant for most occasions. For the best people watching and California ambiance, try to grab a seat on the outdoor patio.

🕐 1100–2300 daily, Weekday HH: 1500–1800
🏠 8905 Melrose Ave., CA 90069
📞 +1 (323) 978 2170 URL graciasmadreweho.com
📎 Check website for special holiday hours

"This restaurant boasts an incredible patio complete with 80-year-old transplanted olive trees and, in true LA fashion, a devoted celebrity following."

– Heather McGinn, ALLTHATISSOLID

40 POT @The Line
Map R, P.106

With good food and characters in abundance, POT serves as a new anchor for The Line hotel and Koreatown. This hipster Korean fusion cooked up by Roy Choi lives up to its reputation. Choi first made a name for himself in the LA food scene with his now famous Korean barbecue taco truck 'Kogi'. POT mainly serves Korean style one pot stew, which comes in three different sizes meant to satisfy groups of two to five. Other standouts include Jalapeño squid and seafood dishes. They also offer crafty Soju-based cocktails, so head over for an all around Korean experience.

🕐 Bar food: 1430–2300 daily,
Dinner: 1700–2300 daily
🏠 3515 Wilshire Blvd, CA 90010
📞 +1 (213) 368 3030
URL www.eatatpot.com

"Reservations are for suckers at this noisy, popular, hipster Korean-fusion dining room. Show up, put your name down and drink at the hotel bar while you wait."

– Eve Speciall

41 Night + Market Song

Map H, P.101

Night + Market Song is as much a place to go for drinks as it is a place for authentic food. The bright interior decorations match the flavor of the food. Chef Kris Yenbamroong presents his version of Thai street food and home cooking. Many dishes are very spicy, so check with the staff if you need milder options. Try their strip club fried rice, and for the more adventurous foodies out there, make sure not to miss the raw blood soup. First come first served, so do come hungry but not too hungry.

🕐 1200–1500 (M–F), 1700–2230 (M–Th), 1700–2300 (F–Sa)
🏠 3322 W. Sunset Blvd., CA 90026
📞 +1 (323) 665 5899
URL www.nightmarketla.com

"Come here for unusual Thai or Los Angeles fusion with amazing wines."

– Nite Jewel

42 **Town Pizza**
Map B, P.99

Located on a busy street of Highland Park, this unmissable crimson red building serves as the hub for Town Pizza. The restaurant serves New York City style pizza with an LA twist. Made with fresh and organic ingredients, they also offer gluten free and vegan cheese options. Town Molé, one of their signature pizzas, pays tribute to the neighborhood. Made with all locally sourced ingredients, this roast pork and molé sauce based pizza gets topped with fresh green cilantro and pink pickled onions.

🕐 1600–2300 (M-F), 1200– (Sa-Su)
🏠 5101 York Blvd. at Ave. 51, CA, 90042
📞 +1 (323) 344 8696 **URL** www.townla.com

"Great new pizza place in Highland Park. Classic thin crust pizza, try the Mole pizza it's amazing."

– Sean Pecknold

43 Taqueria El Tapatio
Map T, P.107

This Glendale hole in the wall will satisfy your late night cravings after a night on the town. The tiny Mexican establishment packs in a loyal following both day and night. Authentic and no fuss, the cash-only restaurant prepares a satisfying assortment of tacos, burritos, and quesadillas served by friendly staff. Pile on the radishes and spicy carrots and be wary of the limited parking during peak rush times.

🕐 1000–0230 (Su-Th), –0330 (F-Sa)
🏠 1266 S. Glendale Ave., CA 91205
📞 +1 (818) 549 4167
🔗 Cash only

"Best chicken quesadillas."
– Isaac Franco & Sean Guerin, De Lux

Kaldi Coffee
Map A, P.99

A simple and tiny storefront on the Atwater strip brews up high quality drip coffee to a dedicated local following. The unpretentious and minimally decorated café has space for just a few tables and communal outdoor seating. If you are lucky, grab one of these rare spots and enjoy the free wifi and casual atmosphere. Otherwise, order your espresso to go and take a stroll along the always charming Glendale Boulevard.

🕐 0630–2000 (M–F), 0730– (Sa–Su)
🏠 3147 Glendale Blvd., CA 90039
📞 +1 (323) 660 6005
URL www.kaldicoffeeatwater.com

"Atwater is the most neighborhood-y of neighborhoods in LA, so if you like that small town feel, this is your spot."
– Molly Cranna

45 Animal Restaurant
 Map L, P.103

Four doors down from the celebrated Canter's Deli and next door to the Supreme skate shop, an unmarked restaurant maintains its immense popularity through word of mouth. The restaurant serves up fine dining in a relaxed atmosphere. True to its name, the establishment offers a tantalizing menu for the carnivorously inclined. Try not to overthink it and just dive right in to the plate of pig ears, veal tongue, or fried rabbit legs. For the less culinarily adventurous, try their sister location Son of a Gun.

🕐 1800–2300 (Su-Th), –0000 (F-Sa)
🏠 435 N. Fairfax Ave., CA 90036
📞 +1 (323) 782 9225
URL animalrestaurant.com
🔖 Reservation required

"They specialize in using all parts of an animal to create unique dishes."

– Kirsten Lepore

 Edendale
Map A, P.99

This relaxing Eastside restaurant and bar gives a historic, turn of the century Los Angeles Fire station a second life. Drawing culinary influences from Southern cuisine to more exotic Asian, Latin American, and Mediterranean dishes, the establishment attracts a lively crowd throughout the day and evening. Whether seated under the impressive old word skylight at the bar or soaking up the sun on the patio, guests will be hard pressed to find a bad spot or dish in the house.

 🕐 1100–1500 (Su), 1700–2200 (Su–W), –2300 (Th–Sa), Bar: 1700–0200 (M–Sa), 1100– (Su) 🏠 2838 Rowena Ave., CA 90039 📞 +1 (323) 666 2000 URL www.theedendale.com

"Great music, if you are into the 90s era 4AD sound."
– Dustin Edward Arnold

47 El Huarachito
Map S, P.106

El Huarachito has been run by the same family for more than half a century and consistently delivers tasty Mexican food. Arrive at the art-clad premises as early as 7am and you'll be treated to a broad range of excellent homestyle options, most of them under $10. Breakfast offers many of the most popular dishes. Try the huevos rancheros served with crispy homemade tortilla chips, two eggs, and topped with a spicy red sauce. It's Mexican home cooking at its finest.

0700-1700 (W–M), –1500 (Tu)
3010 N. Broadway, CA 90031
+1 (323) 223 0476   Cash only

"Don't expect a hipster scene, but for family style Mexican it's all good, especially the Nopales Con Huevo and Melon Aguas Fresca."

– Benjamin Ball, Ball-Nogues Studio

48 Speranza
Map A, P.98

Founded by a former architect from OMA, this Silver Lake Italian restaurant is attracting more and more loyal visitors who appreciates home cooked classic dishes. The moderately priced local establishment incorporates a wine box designed by artist Jorge Pardo. A lush patio, hidden behind an orange welder's curtain, presents a charming atmosphere for enjoying the unpretentious yet sophisticated fair. Chat over a plate of homemade pasta and make sure to save room for the tiramisu at the end of the night.

🕐 1800–0000 (M–Sa), 1700– (Su)
🏠 2547 Hyperion Ave., CA 90027
📞 +1 (323) 644 1918

"This is the local trattoria of the architecture and art crowd, at least for the east side of Los Angeles."
– Barbara Bestor, Bestor Architecture

Nightlife

Hidden cocktail bars, live burlesque shows, and arcade games night

Angelenos may know how to work hard but they also are the masters of unwinding. Whether cutting up the dance floor or frequenting the latest speakeasy, locals maintain an active and eclectic nightlife far removed from the cliché Hollywood club scene. A burgeoning mixology culture and love of all things old fashioned culminates in two of the city's most reliable 1920s style speakeasies: The Roger Room (#51) and Varnish (#53). Those looking for a little music with their cocktail will enjoy the outdoor patio at Villains Tavern (*1356 Palmetto St, CA 90013*), the Wednesday night ragtime band at 1642 beer and wine bar (#52), and the Dresden's king and queen of jazz standards (#56), Marty and Elayne. Depending on your mood, spend the evening admiring the acrobatic burlesque offerings at the charmingly seedy Jumbo's Clown Room (#50) or get away from it all on a midnight hike up to Mount Wilson (#60). The beauty of LA nightlife thrives in its uncanny ability to defy expectation. No matter if you happen to find yourself in the enchanting, invite-only Magic Castle (#59), at the Low End Theory weekly beats party (*2419 N Broadway, CA 90031*) or Sarcastic Disco by DJ Harvey (*www.harveysarcasticdisco.com*), you'll be hard pressed to not have a good time.

Paul Dini
Writer & producer

I'm a comics writer and animation producer. LA's a great city especially if you get off the beaten path and do your own exploring. Have a great time and keep your eyes open!

Jumbo's Clown Room P.087

Lauren Schuchman
Sales rep, The Sweet Shop

I'm the Head of West Coast Sales at The Sweet Shop. As a born and raised native I'm still discovering things here. They say NYC is tough to navigate, but here, you have to seek things out.

Richard Blake
Visual designer

I explore visuals and create innovative and dynamic solutions through art direction, branding, editorial and product design.

El Capitan Theatre P.086

The Roger Room P.088

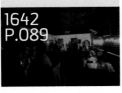

HOLYCHILD
Musician

We are Liz and Louie. We've been exploring LA ever since we moved here two years ago. Honored to share some of our favorite haunts in the city that so hugely informs our art.

The Varnish P.090

John Boiler
Co-founder & CEO, 72andSunny

Co-founder of an advertising agency, who wants to make a huge impact in culture. We reside in the old Howard Hughes executive offices co-opted into an area dubbed "Silicon Beach".

David Altobelli
Writer & film director

I live in Echo Park. I've directed a bunch of music videos and ads among other things that distract me from what I want to be doing, which is to make movies.

1642 P.089

Jon Brion @Largo P.091

Carrie Lau & Lulu Biazus
Art directors & designers, THING

The duo leads multidisciplinary studio THING, which works in a variety of creative areas such as art direction, illustration, graphic design and video art direction.

EightyTwo Arcade Bar P.092

The Dresden P.093

Ruben Hickman
Art director, Paramount Pictures

I've worked on Shrek, Madagascar, and the recent SpongeBob movie. My artistic focus has been on light in color and the creation of wild imaginative worlds.

Amber Quintero
Singer, Boardwalk

I'm Amber Quintero. I've been in LA for almost ten years. I sing in a band called Boardwalk, which also contains Mike Edge. You can find me at the Farmers' Market on Sunday morning.

Crystal Spa P.094

Kagan Taylor & Justin Rice
Owners, Knowhow Shop

An architectural design–build collaboration founded on the duo's interests in digital fabrication and traditional technique. Their work blends a feral strangeness with humor and craft.

The Hermosillo (Highland Park Brewery) P.095

The Magic Castle P.096

Douglas Little
Installation artist & designer

I am a visual installation artist and product designer with a passion for nature, surrealism and extraordinary beauty.

Kimberly & Nancy Wu
Founders, Building Block

The sisters established Building Block in 2011 to re-address daily accessories, edit out the typical excesses of luxury goods while magnifying functional essentials.

Mount Wilson P.097

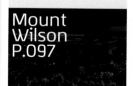

49 El Capitan Theatre
Map J, P.102

Owned and operated by The Walt Disney Company, this meticulously restored 1920s movie palace preserves its original splendor. The family friendly theater screens exclusively Disney and Pixar films with gallery exhibits paired with the latest releases. A giant Wurlitzer organ sweeps guests into a carefree setting with its medley of Disney theme songs. If you are bringing kids along, make sure to catch the frequent pre-shows where Mickey, Minnie, and other costumed Disney characters lead the audience in spirited sing-alongs.

🏠 6838 Hollywood Blvd., CA 90028
🕐 Ticketing: 1 (800) 347 6396
URL elcapitantheatre.com

"If you see no other movie theater in Hollywood, make sure you visit the El Cap."

– Paul Dini

 **50 Jumbo's Clown Room**
Map E, P.100

Wrap up your evening with a trip to Jumbo's Clown Room. This Hollywood institution keeps it classy with some of the most athletic burlesque dancers around. Cheap drinks and eclectic music set a lively atmosphere. The tastefully covered up dancers defy gravity night after night as they spend more time on the ceiling than on the pole. Bring some dollar bills and try to grab a spot next to Lemmy from Motörhead at the bar.

🕐 1600–0200 daily
🏠 5153 Hollywood Blvd., CA 90027
📞 +1 (323) 666 1187 **URL** jumbos.com

"The dancers talk to the audience like you've been friends for years. They also pick their own music from ZZ Top to Morrissey to Nine Inch Nails to Wham!"

– Lauren Schuchman, The Sweet Shop

51 The Roger Room
Map K, P.102

This impeccably elegant and tiny bar captures the spirit of the 1920s speakeasy. With only the obscure neon sign of an old psychic parlor to mark the entry, the bar stays completely out of sight and hidden behind velvet curtains. The high-end mixology bar serves sophisticated cocktails topped with cheeky imprints of skulls, Hello Kitty, and lighting bolts. Circus murals and framed portraits of freak show oddities grant the space a vintage carnivalesque quality. Open daily and reservations accepted.

🕐 1800–0200 (M–F), 1900– (Sa), 2000– (Su)
🏠 370 N. La Cienega Blvd., CA 90048
📞 +1 (310) 854 1300
URL www.therogerroom.com

"The perfect blend of high end speakeasy and neighborhood dive bar."
– Richard Blake

1642
Map I, P.101

This hidden Westlake gem proves as classic as it does understated. A discreet sign and the building number serve as the only clues for finding one's way into this memorable jazz bar. The dark space with exposed brick crafts a perfect date night ambiance. The timeless atmosphere and diverse clientele make this bar one of LA's best kept and most inviting secrets. Stroll in on the right night, you'll find a live swing band, sometimes accompanied by a tap dancer, among other acts.

🕐 1800–0200 (Tu–Sa), –0000 (Su)
🏠 1642 W. Temple St., CA 90026
📘 1642 📞 +1 (213) 989 6836

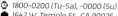

The main attraction is really the vibe and the people you will meet. Go on a Wednesday night, where an amazing ragtime jazz band will play you back into the 1930s."

– HOLYCHILD

53 The Varnish
Map P, P.104

A charming speakeasy nestles behind the legendary Cole's restaurant, home of the French dip sandwich. Guests must walk through the saloon-like establishment and to an unmarked door in the back to reach this timeless bar. Dimly lit and cozy, the wooden booths and classic cocktails whisk patrons away to a simpler time far from the downtown hustle and bustle. Drop by for live jazz nights Sunday, Monday, and Tuesday after 9pm. Cocktail attire not required but always admired.

🕐 1900–0200 daily
🏠 118 E. 6th St., CA 90014
☎ +1 (213) 622 9999
URL www.thevarnishbar.com
🔗 Walk-in only, maximum group of 6

"Ok, so it's a little bit of a disneyland period piece of hipster chic, but the cocktails are worth the pose, the wait, and the cash."
– John Boiler, 72andSunny

54 Jon Brion @Largo

Map K, P.102

John Brion, the master of the movie soundtrack, gives an unpredictably delightful performance once a month at Largo – a nightclub and cabaret on La Cienega. The freeform and engaging show highlights Brion's musical talent as he fluidly moves through a broad range of instruments. The intimate venue inspires audience participation. Varying dramatically from month to month, Brion regularly invites special guests to perform with him on stage. The reasonably priced tickets can be bought in advance online.

⏰ 2130- (Monthly 3rd Fridays) 💲 $30
🏠 366 N. La Cienega Blvd., CA 90048
📞 +1 (310) 855 0350 🔗 www.largo-la.com
✎ Seat assignments begin at 6pm, first-come-first-served. No late entry.

"He plays some of the greats from movies he's scored (Eternal Sunshine, Synechdoche) and also takes requests from the crowd."

– David Altobelli

091

55 EightyTwo Arcade Bar
Map Q, P.105

Far away from the flashy glamorous scene that visitors often associate LA with, this unpretentious arcade bar will transport you back to the 80s when video games were played with fire buttons and joysticks. Just opened in 2014, the ample space now houses over 40 kinds of classic addictive arcade games and pinball machines, including Ms. Pac-Man, Space Invaders, and Teenage Mutant Ninja Turtles. Enjoy a couple of drinks at their crafty cocktail bar with loud game noise or nightly DJ music at the outdoor patio. A free pinball league happens on Tuesdays.

🕐 1800–0200 (Tu–Th), 1700– (F), 1400– (Sa–Su) 🏠 707 E, 4th Pl., CA 90031 📞 +1 (213) 626 8200
URL eightytwo.la 🔞 21+

"This new spot downtown houses a wide range of vintage games and a creative cocktail bar. A cool place to meet and mingle with new and old friends."
– Carrie Lau & Lulu Biazus, THING

56 The Dresden
Map E, P.100

Little has changed in this lively bar and old fashioned restaurant since its opening in 1954. Nestled between hip boutiques, this tried and true establishment preserves an authentic atmosphere enhanced by a loyal following of quirky customers. Sidle up to the piano bar and call out requests to the jazz standard power couple, Marty and Elayne during their nightly sets each Tuesday through Sunday. The tireless energy and tremendous charm of these classic lounge performers is not to be missed.

🕐 Dinner: 1630–2300 daily, lounge: –0200 (M–Sa), –0000 (Su) 🏠 1760 N. Vermont Ave., CA 90027
📞 +1 (323) 665 4294 URL www.thedresden.com

"In many ways it's the beating heart of Los Feliz and my favorite bar since as long as I can remember."
– Ruben Hickman, Paramount Pictures

57 Crystal Spa
Map R, P.106

Nurse your hangover or simply treat yourself at Crystal Spa, an Aveda concept spa in Kore-atown. Book a treatment or enjoy their unlimited access to pools and steam rooms with just a minimal admission fee. In *Jimjilbang*, Korean for "steam room", guests can relax and purify their bodies at any of the four rooms filled with heated Himalayan salt, air purifying charcoal, Korean mud or chilly air. Service menu features include acupressure, facials, body treatments, manicures, and pedicures.

🕐 0600–1200 (Su–M), –0100 (Tu–Th), 24 hrs (F–Sa)
🏠 #321, City Center on 6th, 3500 W. 6th St, CA 90020 📞 +1 (213) 487 5600 🔗 crystalspala.com

"Bars close at 2am in LA but the Korean spa stays open all night! Boys and girls can relax together in the co-ed jimjilbang."
– Amber Quintero, Boardwalk

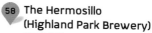

58 The Hermosillo
(Highland Park Brewery)
Map B, P.99

The cheers of Highland Park offers up a daily selection of first-rate craft beers and boutique wines. The inviting brewery and wine bar maintains a cozy atmosphere, complete with professional service and top notch culinary offerings to soak up the alcohol. Get there early to grab one of the coveted booths against the side wall. From there, enjoy the people watching and lively locals over the top of your glass.

🕐 1700–0200 (M–Th), 1200– (F–Su)
🏠 5125 York Blvd., CA 90042
📞 +1 (323) 739 6459
URL www.thehermosillo.com

"Predictably it can get crowded, but tasting a beer from the in-house Highland Park Brewery makes the experience well worth it! Go early and often."

– Kagan Taylor & Justin Rice, Knowhow Shop

59 The Magic Castle

Map J, P.102

True to its name, the mecca of magic never disappoints. Arguably the most prestigious magic fraternity in the world, the invitation-only establishment occupies a grand Victorian mansion in the Hollywood Hills. Once inside, guests and elite magicians alike may explore various magic shows, grab a cocktail, or stay for dinner. Ask around for an invitation, it is worth the effort. Come early and snag a seat for the up-close magic show. Brave ones should test their courage by visiting Misty Lee's Seance Room. Black tie only.

🕐 Show time vary with program   🏠 7001 Franklin Ave., CA 90028-8600   ☎ +1 (323) 851 3313
🌐 www.magiccastle.com   🖇 Trial membership: $250 for 30 days, bring up to 8 each visit. Dinning compulsory. 21+ except Saturday brunch.

"The environment is laced with magic ephemera and wonderful little bars where you can perch and pickle yourself prior to being mystified."

– Douglas Little

60 Mount Wilson
Map AE, P.109

Few spots in the city can compete with Mount Wilson's panoramic views. Spanning from past downtown to the ocean, the vistas visible here will impress even the most skeptical of hearts. This scenic peak in the San Gabriel Mountains encompasses part of the Angeles National Forest. For those that feel like star gazing, the Mount Wilson Observatory offers guided tours on Saturdays and Sundays. Bring a picnic or grab some lunch at the observatory's Cosmic Café.

🕐 *Observatory: 1000-1700 daily (Apr to Nov, weather permitting)* 📞 *+1 (404) 413 5484* URL *www.mtwilson.edu* 🔗 *National Forest Adventure Pass or Golden Age Passport needed for parking, obtainable from Shell stations or Cosmic Café at the observatory.*

"If somehow you find yourself in LA on the 4th of July, go here to see all of LA's fireworks from one spot at one time."

– Kimberly & Nancy Wu, Building Block

MAP A

- 23_Philosophical Research Society
- 48_Speranza

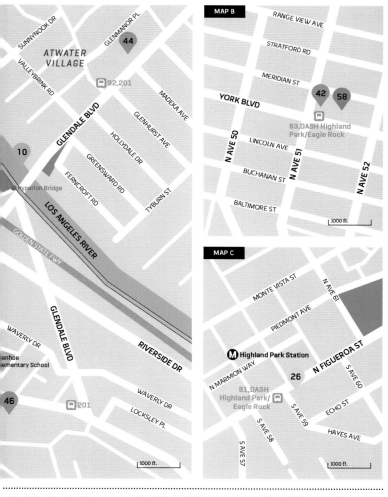

- 10_Los Angeles River
- 26_Mount Analog
- 42_Town Pizza
- 44_Kaldi Coffee
- 46_Edendale
- 58_The Hermosillo (Highland Park Brewery)

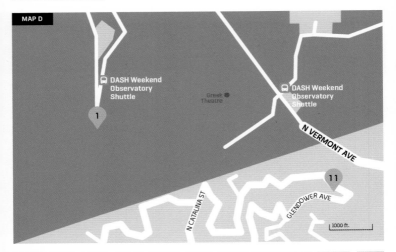

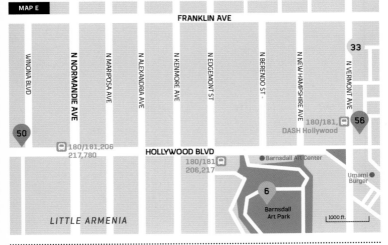

- 1_Griffith Observatory
- 6_Hollyhock House
- 11_Ennis House
- 33_Skylight Books
- 50_Jumbo's Clown Room
- 56_The Dresden Lounge

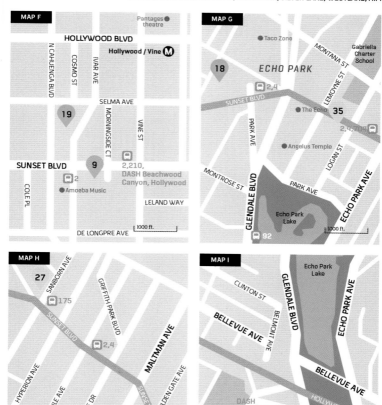

- 9_Cinerama Dome
- 18_Machine Project
- 19_Space 15 Twenty
- 27_Mohawk General Store
- 35_Time Travel Mart
- 41_Night + Market Song
- 52_1642

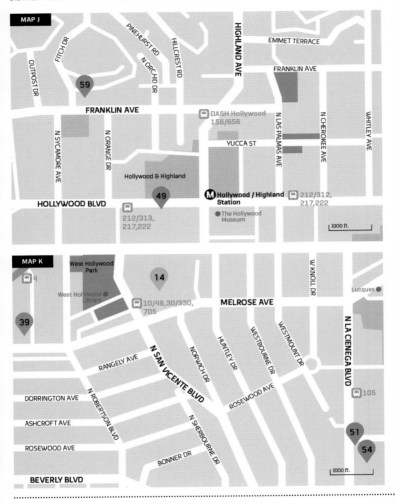

- 14_MOCA (Design Pacific Centre)
- 39_Gracias Madre
- 49_El Capitan Theatre
- 51_The Roger Room
- 54_Jon Brion @Largo
- 59_The Magic Castle

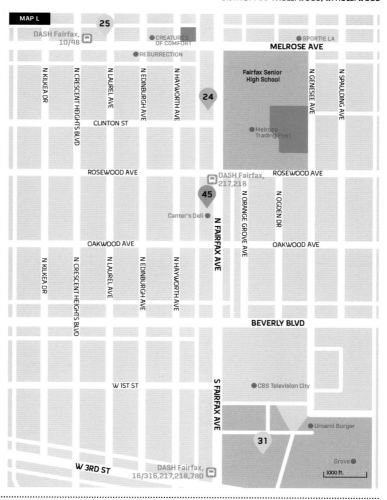

MAP L

DASH Fairfax, 10/48

25

CREATURES OF COMFORT

RESURRECTION

SPORTIE LA

MELROSE AVE

Fairfax Senior High School

N KILKEA DR

N CRESCENT HEIGHTS BLVD

N LAUREL AVE

N EDINBURGH AVE

N HAYWORTH AVE

N GENESEE AVE

N SPAULDING AVE

CLINTON ST

24

Melrose Trading Post

ROSEWOOD AVE

ROSEWOOD AVE

DASH Fairfax, 217,218

45

Canter's Deli

N ORANGE GROVE AVE

N OGDEN DR

OAKWOOD AVE

OAKWOOD AVE

N FAIRFAX AVE

BEVERLY BLVD

W 1ST ST

S FAIRFAX AVE

CBS Television City

Umami Burger

31

Grove

1000 ft.

DASH Fairfax, 16/316,217,218,780

W 3RD ST

- 24_The Cinefamily
- 25_Melrose Avenue
- 31_The Original Farmers Market
- 45_Animal Restaurant

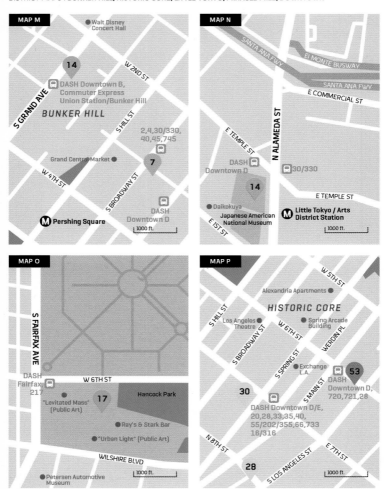

- 7_Bradbury Building
- 14M_MOCA (Grand Avenue)
- 14N_MOCA (Greffen Contemporary)
- 17_LACMA
- 28_69 Showroom
- 30_California Millinery Supply Company
- 53_The Varnish

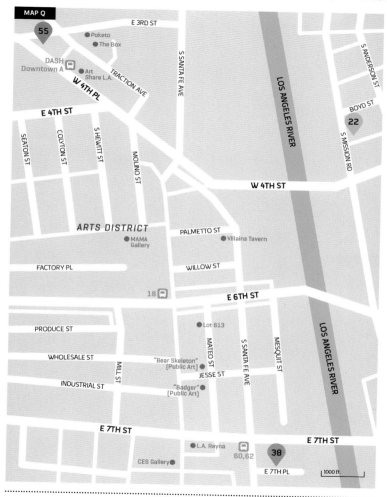

MAP Q

55

E 3RD ST

● Poketo
● The Box

DASH
Downtown A
● Art
Share L.A.

TRACTION AVE

W 4TH PL

W 4TH ST

E 4TH ST

S SANTA FE AVE

LOS ANGELES RIVER

S ANDERSON ST

BOYD ST

22

S MISSION RD

SEATON ST

COLYTON ST

S HEWITT ST

MOLINO ST

W 4TH ST

ARTS DISTRICT

PALMETTO ST

● MAMA
Gallery

● Villains Tavern

FACTORY PL

WILLOW ST

18

E 6TH ST

PRODUCE ST

● Lot 613

MATEO ST

S SANTA FE AVE

MESQUIT ST

LOS ANGELES RIVER

WHOLESALE ST

MILL ST

"Bear Skeleton"
[Public Art] ●

INDUSTRIAL ST

JESSE ST

"Badger" ●
[Public Art]

E 7TH ST

E 7TH ST

● L.A. Reyna

60,62

38

CES Gallery ●

E 7TH PL

1000 ft.

● 22_356 Mission
● 38_Bestia
● 55_EightyTwo Arcade Bar

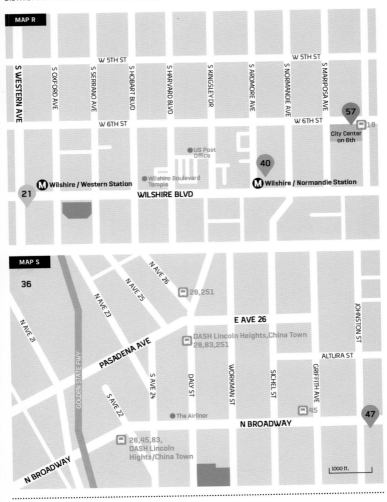

MAP R

W 5TH ST

W 5TH ST

S WESTERN AVE
S OXFORD AVE
S SERRANO AVE
S HOBART BLVD
S HARVARD BLVD
S KINGSLEY DR
S ARDMORE AVE
S NORMANDIE AVE
S MARIPOSA AVE

W 6TH ST

W 6TH ST

57

18

City Center
on 6th

US Post
Office

40

Wilshire Boulevard
Temple

Ⓜ Wilshire / Western Station

Ⓜ Wilshire / Normandie Station

21

WILSHIRE BLVD

MAP S

36

N AVE 26

N AVE 25

N AVE 23

N AVE 21

28,251

E AVE 26

JOHNSTON ST

DASH Lincoln Heights,China Town
28,83,251

PASADENA AVE

ALTURA ST

GOLDEN STATE FWY

S AVE 24

S AVE 22

DALY ST

WORKMAN ST

SICHEL ST

GRIFFITH AVE

45

47

The Airliner

N BROADWAY

28,45,83,
DASH Lincoln
Hights/China Town

1000 ft.

N BROADWAY

- 21_The Wiltern
- 36_St. Vincent de Paul Store
- 40_POT @The Line
- 47_El Huarachito
- 57_Crystal Spa

MAP T

E CHEVY CHASE DR

E PALMER AVE

S GLENDALE AVE

S BRAND BLVD

S MARYLAND AVE

90/91

43

90/91

E CYPRESS ST

E LOS FELIZ RD

1000 ft.

MAP U

SANTA MONICA BLVD

West Hollywood
City Council

ROMAINE ST

N CROFT AVE

N ORLANDO AVE

N KINGS RD

N SWEETZER AVE

WILLOUGHBY AVE

4

Cityline East bound
Orange Route/
West Bound Blue Route

WARING AVE

1000 ft.

MAP V

LOMBARDY RD

S ALLEN AVE

ORLANDO RD

MAUSOLEUM RD

DR PALM

S BOUND DR

2

GRAY DR

1000 ft.

MAP W

BROADWAY ST

WESTMINSTER AVE

6TH AVE

SAN JUAN AVE

SANTA CLARA AVE

CALIFORNIA AVE

ELECTRIC AVE

29

1 ABBOT KINNEY BLVD 1

CABRILLO AVE

ALHAMBRA CT

Gjelina

RIVIERA AVE

WINDWARD AVE

ANDALUSIA AVE

CORDOVA CT

RIALTO AVE

1000 ft.

- 2_The Huntington Gardens
- 4_Schindler House
- 29_Tortoise General Store
- 43_Taqueria El Tapatio

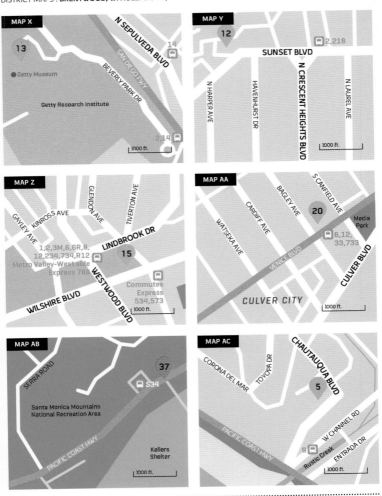

- ● 5_Eames House
- ● 12_Chateau Marmont
- ● 13_The Getty Center
- ● 15_Hammer Museum
- ● 20_The Museum of Jurassic Technology
- ● 37_Malibu Farm

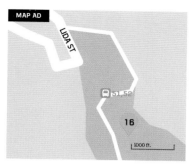

MAP AD

LIDA ST

🚌 51, 52

16

1000 ft.

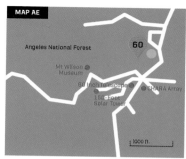

MAP AE

Angeles National Forest

60

Mt Wilson
Museum

60 Inch Telescope

CHARA Array

150-Foot
Solar Tower

1000 ft.

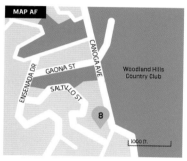

MAP AF

CANOGA AVE

ENSENADA DR

GAONA ST

SALTILLO ST

Woodland Hills
Country Club

8

1000 ft.

MAP AG

MOORPARK ST

MAMMOTH AVE

WOODMAN AVE

VENTURA CANYON AVE

VENTURA BLVD

150/240, 🚌
158, 750

34

1000 ft.

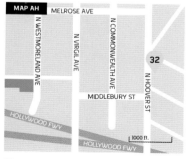

MAP AH

MELROSE AVE

N WESTMORELAND AVE

N VIRGIL AVE

N COMMONWEALTH AVE

N HOOVER ST

32

MIDDLEBURY ST

HOLLYWOOD FWY

HOLLYWOOD FWY

1000 ft.

MAP AI

SILVER LAKE BLVD

EDGEWATER TERRACE

GLENDALE BLVD

3

Silver Lake
Meadow

🚌 92

Silver Lake
Reservoir

1000 ft.

● 3_Neutra VDL Studio &
Residences

● 8_Al Struckus House

● 16_Art Center College
of Design

● 32_Old Style Guitar Shop

● 34_Freakbeat Records

● 60_Mount Wilson

109

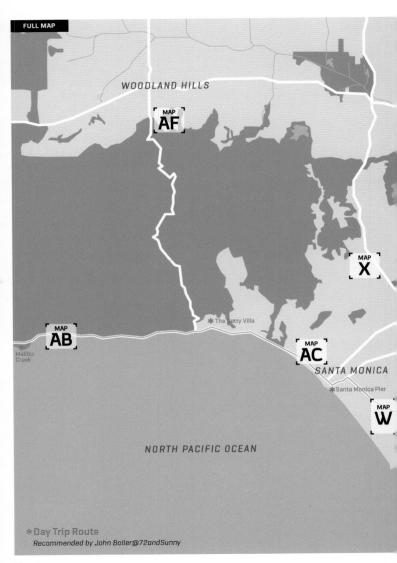

FULL MAP

WOODLAND HILLS

MAP
AF

MAP
X

MAP
AB

Malibu
Creek

✳ The Getty Villa

MAP
AC

SANTA MONICA

✳ Santa Monica Pier

MAP
W

NORTH PACIFIC OCEAN

✳ Day Trip Route
Recommended by John Boiler@72andSunny

110

N NUYS

BURBANK

GLENDALE

SHERMAN OAKS

MAP AG

MAP AE

MAP AD

MAP V

MAP T

Hollywood Sign

MAP D

MAP A

MAP B

MAP C

MAP Y

MAP J

MAP E

MAP F

MAP H

MAP AI

MAP G

MAP S

MAP K

MAP U

MAP L

MAP AH

BEVERLY HILLS

MAP O

MAP R

MAP M

MAP N

MAP P

MAP Q

MAP AA

CULVER CITY

HUNTINGTON PARK

INGLEWOOD

Los Angeles International Airport

El Segundo

Accommodations

Hip hostels, fully-equipped apartments & swanky hotels

No journey is perfect without a good night's sleep to recharge. Whether you're backpacking or on a business trip, our picks combine top quality and convenience, whatever your budget.

($) < $100   **($)** $101–250   **($)** $251+

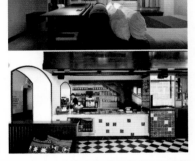

Ace Hotel Downtown LA

Ace Hotel's new branch in LA occupies the historic United Artists theater building built in 1927. Check in to experience Spanish Gothic details, Schindler-inspired rooms and voguish works of art all layered in one. Bask in the Angeleno sun at the rooftop pool or on one of Ace's Tokyo-bikes for free. Valet parking costs $36 per night.

🏠 929 S. Broadway, CA 90015   📞 +1 (213) 623 3233   **URL** www.acehotel.com/losangeles   **($)**

The Line

Drawing inspiration from the dynamic Kore-
atown district, the Line has a lot going on. The
fully renovated 388-room hotel is a collaboration
by the Sydell Group with chef Roy Choi, designer
Sean Knibb, lifestyle store Poketo, artists and
Linus Bikes. Floor to ceiling windows in each
room command the stunning city view.

 3515 Wilshire Blvd., CA 90010
+1 (213) 368 7411 URL thelinehotel.com

Palihotel Melrose

Palihotel is designed for urban explorers who value functionality and details. Its convenient position on Melrose Avenue means you'll have a raft of chic boutiques, theaters and a farmers' market on your doorstep. Palihotel's new lavish suites and selected Queen rooms boast private balconies or verandas.

🏠 7950 Melrose Ave., CA 90046
📞 +1 (323) 272 4588 URL pali-hotel.com

One Fine Stay

Like a more polished concept of Airbnb, One Fine Stay offers fully furnished and serviced apartments across LA, ranging from canal-side bungalows in Venice to architectural homes in the Hollywood Hills. Look for the ideal house by checking your personal demands, whether it's for a family or single traveller with a pet. Professional staff are on tap 24/7.

☎ +1 (310) 594 7478 URL onefinestay.com

Jerry's Motel

🏠 285 Lucas Ave., CA 90026
📞 +1 (213) 481 8181
URL www.jerrysmotel.com

Palihouse West Hollywood

🏠 8465 Holloway Dr., CA 90069
📞 +1 (323) 656 4100
URL www.palihouse.com

The Charlie Hotel

🏠 819 N Sweetzer Ave., CA 90069
📞 +1 (323) 988 9000
URL thecharliehotel.com

Notes

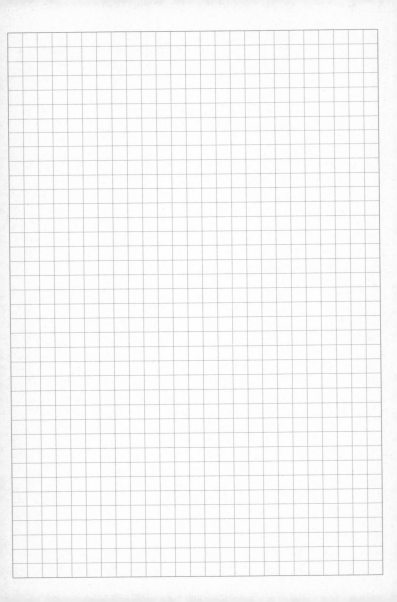

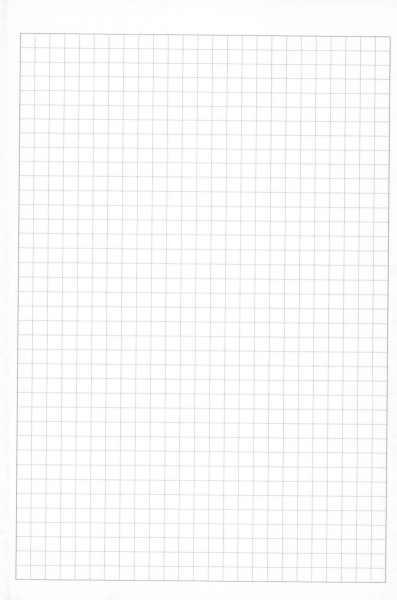

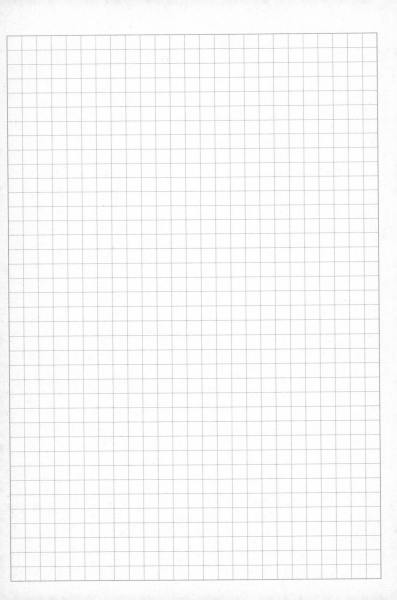

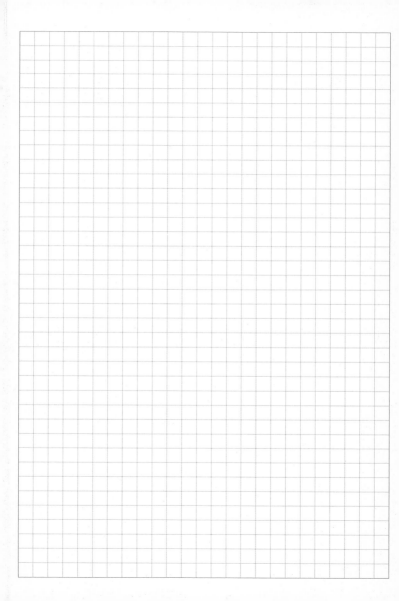

Index

Multimedia

Kirsten Lepore, p078
www.kirstenlepore.com

Music

Amber Quintero @Boardwalk, p094
Soundcloud.com/BoardwalkLa

Danny Boy O'Connor @House of Pain & La Coka Nostra, p026
FB: Delta Bravo Urban Exploration Team

Darren Weiss @PAPA, p061
Papatheband.com
Portrait by Sam Monkarsh

De Lux, p076
FB: deluxband

Eve Speciall, p073
evespeciall.com
Portrait by Kevin McShane

HOLYCHILD, p089
www.holychildmusic.com

Hrishikesh Hirway, p032
hrishikeshhirway.com

Leland Jackson aka Ahnnu, p041
www.dogtropic.net

Lo-fang, p014
lo-fang.com

Nico Stai, p044
www.nicostai.com

Nite Jewel, p074
www.nitejewel.com
Portrait by Angel Ceballos

Photography

Aleks Kocev, p034
alekskocev.com

Gina Clyne, p025
www.ginaclyne.com

Hugh Kretschmer, p058
www.hughkretschmer.net

MI-ZO, p018
www.mi-zo.com

Molly Cranna, p077
www.mollycranna.com

Photo & other credits

69 Showroom, p055
(Interior) 69 Showroom

Animal Restaurant, p078
(All) Animal Restaurant

Art Center College of Design, p036
(Signage) Crystal Jean Photography, (p37 exhibition wide view) cspangler (p.37 workshop) Art Center College of Design

Bestia, p070
(Interior during service p070 & pizza p071) Erik Sun, (dish p070) Sierra Prescott, (p071) Andrea Bricco, (others) Courtesy of Bestia

Crystal Spa, p094
(All) Courtesy of Crystal Spa

Eames House, p020
(All) Courtesy of Eames Office, LLC

Ennis House, p026
(Middle & bottom) jalbertgagnier on Flickr

Gracias Madre, p072
(Exterior) Kelly Brown, (Interior) Eric Wolfinger

Griffith Observatory, p014
(All) Griffith Observatory, (p.14 top exterior) Friends of The Observatory, Justin Donais, (view) Griffith Observatory Astronomical Observer Anthony Cook

Hollyhock House, p021
(All) Joshua White

Los Angeles River, p025
(All) Creative Commons (CC)

Machine Project, p040
(All) Courtesy of Machine Project

Malibu Farm, p068
(All) Sam McGuire

MOCA, p034
(Exterior) Marissa Roth, (Interior) Installation view of Selections from the Permanent Collection, now on view at MOCA Grand Avenue, photo by Brian Forrest, ©The Museum of Contemporary Art, Los Angeles.

Mount Analog, p053
(All) Courtesy of Mount Analog

Mount Wilson, p097
(All) Bryan Ungard on Flickr

Night + Market Song, p074
(All) Laure Joliet

POT @The Line, p073
(All) Rick Poon

Skylight Books, p060
(Interior) Sam McGuire

Taqueria El Tapatio, p076
(All) Sam McGuire

The Getty Center, p032
(p.33 all) Courtesy of The J. Paul Getty Trust.

The Huntington Gardens, p016
(All) Courtesy of The Huntington Library, Art Collections, and Botanical Gardens

The Museum of Jurassic Technology, p042
(Interior & exhibits except miniature) Museum of Jurassic Technology, (miniature) Jennifer Bastian

The Roger Room, p088
(Bottom interior) Courtesy of The Roger Room

The Varnish, p090
(All) Courtesy of The Varnish

Time Travel Mart, p062
(All) Sam McGuire

Accommodations: all courtesy of respective hotels. The Line: all by Adrian Gaut; Ace: (Bedroom & coffee counter) Spencer Lowell, (Suite) Lauren Coleman.

CITIX60

CITIx60: Los Angeles

First published and distributed by
viction workshop ltd

viction:ary™

7C Seabright Plaza, 9-23 Shell Street,
North Point, Hong Kong

Url: www.victionary.com
Email: we@victionary.com
🅵 www.facebook.com/victionworkshop
🐦 www.twitter.com/victionary_
🐾 www.weibo.com/victionary

Edited and produced by viction:ary

Concept & art direction: Victor Cheung
Research & editorial: Queenie Ho, Caroline Kong, Eunyi Choi
Project coordination: Jovan Lip, Katherine Wong
Layout & district map illustration: Frank Lo

Contributing writer, curator & project coordination: Sofia Borges
Cover map illustration: Josh Evans
Count to 10 illustrations: Guillaume Kashima aka Funny Fun
Photography: Christopher Dimaano

Content is compiled based on facts available as of February 2015. Travellers
are advised to check for updates from respective locations before your visit.

First edition
ISBN 978-988-13203-2-2
Printed and bound in China

Acknowledgements

A special thank you to all creatives, photographer(s), editor, producers, com-
panies and organisations for your crucial contributions to our inspiration and
knowledge necessary for the creation of this book. And, to the many whose
names are not credited but have participated in the completion of the book,
we thank you for your input and continuous support all along.